Ten Things You Don't Know About Rhode Island

The **Rhode Island Policy Reporter**, *founded in 2003, is a newsletter about public policy in Rhode Island, specializing in the technical issues that get little attention but that make a huge difference to all of us. Articles about tax policy, housing markets, pension technicalities, land use, and economics may not sound thrilling, but they are issues that rule our lives.*

*You can subscribe to a free weekly email column or to the newsletter itself, which is published (on actual paper!) on a schedule that, well, let's say it aspires to monthliness. Subscription details are available at **whatcheer.net**.*

Ten Things You Don't Know About Rhode Island

A skeptical look at government, economics and recent history in one lively little state.

Tom Sgouros

Light Publications
Providence

A dedication to my parents, Thomas and Joan Sgouros,
who taught me everything I know about dedication.

Edited by Mark Binder
Design consultation by Beth Hellman
Typeset with LaTeX (memoir class)

Portions of this book were originally published in the *Rhode Island Policy Reporter* and in the *Woonsocket Call*, the *Pawtucket Times* and other RIMG papers. For more information, for subscriptions to the *Policy Reporter*, or a free weekly email column, please visit *http://whatcheer.net*.

ISBN 978-0-9824707-0-1
Printed in the United States of America
10 9 8 7 6 5 4 3 2 1

Light Publications
PO Box 2462
Providence, RI 02906
www.lightpublications.com

Contents

Ten Things You Don't Know About Rhode Island

Rhode Island is in a crisis. Hamstrung by a legislature in thrall to powerful unions and the lobbyists for social service agencies, we have spent far beyond our means. Furthermore, profligate spending by cities and towns is bankrupting local government, and threatens to take the state down, too. Meanwhile, to satisfy the unquenchable demand for government services and benefits, taxes are rising every year without end.

DOES THIS STORY SOUND FAMILIAR? It should. I encounter it in the newspaper, on the internet, on talk radio, and in conversation with my friends. You probably do, too. I think of it as the "conventional tale," and it defines the politics of the past two decades here in Rhode Island. I've heard it not just from friends and neighbors, but from the vast majority of the many legislators, town councilors, school committee members I've ever spoken with.

The problem is that this conventional tale is wrong in nearly every particular. Labor has several allies in the state legislature, but it has lost almost all the high-profile battles it has undertaken over the past decade. Welfare benefits are stingy and hard to get here, just like in other states, and the welfare rolls have declined dramatically over the past dozen years. Meanwhile, few municipalities are spending any more than the bare minimum necessary to meet legal requirements—and the ever-increasing demand for services by their own residents.

1

What about taxes? Aren't Rhode Islanders paying more and more taxes each year? Even this, it turns out, is not correct. If you ignore the take from the Rhode Island Lottery and the video slot terminals in Newport and Lincoln, the proportion of our state's economy collected in state fees and taxes *plus* all local property taxes has barely budged, except to decline slightly since the early 1990's. What's changed is who pays them.

To be clear, Rhode Island and its government have some serious problems, and they demand solutions. But the conventional tale is just wrong. This is important not because I have a more loathsome set of villains to hold responsible for the mess, or because of some abstract standard of fairness I might uphold. It's important because when the analysis of our problems is wrong, the solutions we come up with don't work, and *the problems don't get fixed*. A patient comes to a doctor with a headache. If the doctor misses the brain tumor, then the aspirin he prescribes isn't going to do the job, no matter what his credentials are (or however much health insurance the patient has).

Stories are how we make sense of the world, and the conventional tale is simple and satisfies our craving for villains. It's easy to master the overall outline, and there's a host of detail available that seems to corroborate it. When a town budget doesn't get cut, it's easy to blame it on unions, and when the Assembly can't eliminate welfare, it's easy to blame that on poor people or immigrants. But to take this route is to miss the facts, miss the point, and miss the real story.

There is a better explanation of our crisis, and this book presents what amounts to a second opinion about Rhode Island's condition. The short version is this:

- The pressure to keep taxes down has led to an impressive panoply of poor choices of expenses to cut. Many of the cuts we've seen in the past few years have been to programs and expenses intended to *save* money, such as road and building maintenance, but also programs like Medicaid.

- We've made some popular, but very expensive, spending choices, including mandatory minimum drug sentences, suburban sewers, and a near-doubling of the state's roadway miles, among others.

- Anti-tax pressure has created a glut of inappropriate borrowing, notably at the Department of Transportation, but elsewhere, too. Enormous increases in debt service costs are a major source of our current fiscal crisis.

- We've refused to acknowlege the fiscal pressures on our cities and towns in any way beside the verbal. Many municipalities have made appalling land-use decisions and raised property taxes far beyond the defensible not because they wanted to, but because they felt forced to in order to meet their budgets.

- Suburban growth has created unseen subsidies, which is not a problem so long as the growth continues, but becomes a serious structural issue when the growth stops—as it must.

- Fantasy-based tax policy has driven us to cut state taxes only to see municipalities make up the difference with property taxes. The result has been tax savings for a very small number of people (the wealthy) and large increases on the vast majority of the state (everyone else).

- The recently collapsing global economy has played an obvious part in our woes, but our fiscal crisis was underway long before it began.

What's remarkable is not just that there is a realistic alternate story but that the solutions suggested by the conventional tale often make things worse. For example, political pressures created by that tale have shaped the economy-slowing fiscal policies in place today. Our spending cutbacks and regressive tax policies help depress the state's economy, which in turn exerts a downward pressure on tax revenue, promoting more spending cutbacks (and, curiously, more tax cuts). Another example is the substitution of borrowed bond funding for tax revenue. These are not simply of academic interest; they also help explain the apparent intractability of our crisis.

Rhode Island's problems are a complicated story, and I can't pretend to be complete within the covers of such a short volume, but you'll find within this book a collection of newspaper columns and articles from the *Rhode Island Policy Reporter* that describe many of the pieces of this puzzle. There are pieces describing each of the points above, and others that make the connections among them. The articles are sorted into chapters, though many of them could have fit equally into more than one.[1]

I started the *Reporter* in 2003, to look at the stories that I felt were—and still are—getting short shrift in our public conversation. Some of the stories get little attention because they are about frankly technical issues, others are ignored because they are not controversial, even though they deserve to be.

In several years of research on these stories and others like them, I've learned to appreciate what I think of as the paradox of public policy research in Rhode Island. That is, I'm no longer surprised that almost every rock I turn over has something surprising hiding beneath—and it's usually another blow to the conventional tale.

What are the Ten Things?

I admit it sounds a little arrogant to say that I know ten things about Rhode island that you don't know, but in 2007 I began giving a talk by this title to different audiences around the state. Since then, I've spoken to groups of state legislators and to Rotary club members, to labor unions and even an investment club. I've learned that it's relatively easy to find facts with which no one is familiar.

For most people I know, government and the economy ranks fourth or fifth or lower on the list of things to keep track of— well below family, work, school, refinancing the house, and so on. Some people rank the weather higher, too, but I think most realize these are important issues. Life in the 21st Century is busy, and it's hard to keep up. This is what makes the conventional tale so insidious. Because it is so simple, it creates confidence that you know what's going on, and allows everyone to save time by not looking into these matters.

In part this also represents the priorities of the press. You can watch news about the President and Congress 24/7 on television

---

[1]Where an essay appears in more or less its original form, the month of publication is indicated. Where no month is indicated, the essay has been written for this volume, or has been edited so heavily that it bears little resemblance to the original. Also, links to references mentioned in this book can be found at *whatcheer.net/tenthings*.

Also, I love footnotes, which is where you usually find the best stuff in official reports. I hope readers will forgive me for using them liberally here.

and the internet, and even (for now) from your choice of newspapers. The Rhode Island State House, on the other hand, is covered by a surprisingly small handful of reporters, working for an even smaller handful of media outlets.

So what are these ten things? There's no list here because then you'd say, "I already know numbers five and eight" and you'd feel cheated and call me a bad person. The truth is they're different for each reader. Read on, and if you haven't reached ten things by the end of the book, then I need your help to write articles for the *Rhode Island Policy Reporter*.[2]

Doing this work, I've come to be familiar with a decent-sized chunk of the state budget. The sheer number of moving pieces that make up our state's government and economy make it unlikely that anyone can ever be said to master the whole, even in a small state like ours, so all I can really say is that I've spent a fair amount of time crawling around in the weeds. But I have found some interesting things there, and I hope you'll consider their implications.

By far the most important lesson I've found in my contemplations of those weeds is that in the search for villains, it's important not to look away from the mirror. Like any other state, Rhode Island has its share of rogues. These people certainly don't make government any better—and they make it a lot harder to defend the government when it needs defense—but it is simply too much to imagine our crisis is their doing alone. We have all offered our able assistance in the construction of this crisis, by approving popular but expensive policies, developing land better left vacant, voting for people who only make things worse, and more. It's been a long road getting here, and it will take work to get out, but we're not going to make progress at all until we understand how it all happened.

---

[2]If you found ten new things, then please consider subscribing to the *Reporter*—for number eleven. See *whatcheer.net* for details.

One

The Budget Follies

What are the hard budget choices?

Many state spending programs exist to save money. RIte Care, for example, the Medicaid program for poor people, is more economical than letting poor people be served by hospital emergency rooms. This makes cutting these programs especially hard for reasons that have nothing at all to do with one's philosophical stance about government.

April 2009

WHILE DEBATING THE STATE BUDGET in 2009, Senate Majority Leader Daniel Connors (D-Cumberland,Lincoln) said the budget "doesn't represent the hard choices we're going to have to make." He was apparently referring to the fact that the budget didn't cut enough. You hear this kind of talk about "hard choices" all the time. As if there's anything hard about sticking it to poor people and cities.

What's so hard about it? Suburban legislators like Connors routinely get elected and re-elected by mouthing platitudes about hard choices, tsking piously about the problems of our cities, and by promising to get tough on unions. Legislators who vote for these things still get invited to good parties. They can still raise money for their re-elections and no one throws eggs at them when they speak in public. Life is good.

What's more, they routinely follow through on these promises, this year stripping cities and towns not only of the state aid promised them last June, but also most of the stimulus money granted by Congress and President Obama. In the last few years, the pensions and health benefits for state employees have been cut, teacher unions all across the state have given back health benefits, health care for poor people has been trimmed and cut and pruned. Did you know that the monthly cash benefit for welfare recipients is the same today as it was in 1989?

What provokes people to claim choices are hard is that occasionally they realize these policies may be popular, but are also shortsighted and, well, stupid.

Cutting expenses in the state and municipal budgets is hard for a lot of different reasons. Some expenses are enforceable in courts. These are not only labor contracts (whose enforceability is increasingly under question in Rhode Island), but also commitments to the federal government or to individual citizens. Special education laws, for example, have a thoroughly-worked out series of appeal possibilities that start with committees in a school and can go right up into federal courts. These appeal routes are well charted because the federal money for these federal mandates has never been enough to pay more than about 18% of the expenses. Local school districts have ample incentives to balk at the expenses, and parents have ample incentive to appeal the balking.

Another important reason cutting budgets is hard is because a lot of state policies exist to *save* money. Why do we give health care to poor people? Because overcrowded emergency rooms are more expensive. (Plus it ruins the feng shui of our cities to have people dying in the gutter.) Why do we have free public education? Because in terms of our economy, ignorance is more expensive. Why should we maintain the roads, bridges and properties we own? Because *not* doing the maintenance is far more expensive. All of these policies, and many more, exist because previous generations understood they were important ways to save money.

So what happens when we don't do them? That's easy, things get more expensive and we don't save money. Bob Weygand, the VP of operations at the University of Rhode Island, recently told the campus newspaper that the university has about $400 million in deferred maintenance: windows, roofs, and boilers that need fixing on existing buildings.[1] That's almost an entire year of their operating budget, and more than five times what they get from the state every year, and it's grown a lot recently. According to a faculty gadfly I know, in 1995 the administration estimated the deferred maintenance at $55 million. Anyone who thinks that

---

[1] *The Good Five-cent Cigar*, 8 April 2009, "URI racks up $400M in delayed capital projects, maintenance," Chris Curtis.

problem can be ignored year after year without consequences is dreaming.

The same thing is true in all of our public infrastructure. With your pinky finger you can dislodge hand-size chunks of cement and rusted iron from a bridge near my house. Inspectors come a couple of times a year to track its decay, but there is no prospect for its repair, even with the stimulus money from Washington because other bridges are in worse shape. Big trucks can't use part of Route 95 any more, the most important road in the state, since its bridge over the Seekonk River is so rotted. We're replacing the Sakonnet River Bridge because Department of Transportation (DOT) engineers deem it too far gone to be worth repairing.

The choices are always presented as between raising taxes and cutting services, but it's childish to think it so simple. Your legislators face this choice: On the one hand, they can continue cutting taxes on rich people (more such cuts are in the budget this year), forcing cities and towns to raise property taxes. These cuts will continue to devastate maintenance and other spending programs intended to save money in the future, making our future problems worse, and forcing tax increases to be bigger when some bridge falls down or worse. Meanwhile the increased property taxes will continue to be the most onerous tax for most businesses and people.

On the other hand, legislators could ask the rich to forego the satisfaction of yet another tax cut, and maybe even roll back the recent cuts to the bad old days of, say, 1996. They could use this money to relieve cities and towns of some of the crushing burdens they face, and forestall property tax increases. Who knows, we could even fix some bridges.

I'm sorry to break this news to you, but some taxes will rise whatever the Assembly does with the state budget this year. The question before us isn't whether to cut taxes or not. As I said, that's a childish framing of the question. The real question before us is who pays? Do you want our children to pay, or shall we? Shall we ask people who have the most to share what they have, or demand more from people who have little or none? These are the real questions, though unpopular. The real proof of political courage will be a willingness to ask them, not more yammering about supposedly hard choices.

2007: Half a budget, better than none?

*A history of our budget fiasco. In 1997, I asked Michael O'Keefe,
the chief Fiscal Advisor to the House Finance Committee, whether
he thought phasing out the car tax would be too expensive to do
if the state also passed the income tax cut. His reply was, "The
Chairman [then-Representative Tony Pires of Pawtucket] feels that
the state would benefit from increased fiscal constraints in future
years." Well here we are. Our crisis is a crisis we chose. Here are
some observations from 2007 to convince you.*

March 2007

BUDGET SEASON is upon us again. As is usual in recent years,
there isn't very much to be cheery about, except for the cro-
cuses coming up through the mud. Deep cuts are expected nearly
everywhere in state and local government. But there is a faint
silvery lining to the fiscal clouds this year. The size of the fiscal
shortfall is so dramatic that it is forcing the people in charge to be
honest about the issues, for the first time in years.[2]

Our state is in a terrible fiscal situation this year: revenues
won't meet expenditures for the *current* fiscal year, and they are
even worse next year and the year after. A great deal of the blame
for this situation can be laid at the feet of the people who crafted
our state's budget in recent years. Last spring's budget proceedings were a model of either self-deception or double-talk by all
parties, and a measure of the deception is the size of the current
year deficit: $100 million. The shenanigans did their job, and all
the interested parties were re-elected last fall (in 2006).

The issue is a simple refusal to add up the costs and present
the taxpayers with the bill. For fear that people will be unhappy
about the cost of providing government services, legislators and
governors resort to tricks to put off or hide costs, which ultimately
makes the services much more expensive.

- We routinely borrow for things that ought to be paid for out
  of current expenditures: the Department of Transportation is
  the model here, where we borrow tens of millions of dollars
  every year, come rain or shine.

- We routinely refuse to invest in places where we know we
  could save money in the future: investments in education

---

[2]Ed. note: this was overly optimistic.

and child care mean less money spent on social services and corrections down the road.

- We routinely wait for a crisis before addressing issues of critical policy: water shortages have to happen before people think maybe it would have been good to have preserved a bit more open space for wells when we had a chance.

The Governor's proposed budget for fiscal year 2008 is an astonishing document. It seems to imply he thinks that our state's most pressing fiscal problems can only be solved by someone else. Meanwhile, all we can do is suffer. For example, runaway health care costs are bankrupting the state, as well as our municipalities (not to mention our businesses and citizens). The budget is completely silent on the topic.

The high cost of dealing with the unfunded liabilities of our pension system is a close second place in its effect both on state departments and cities and towns. Again, the budget is silent on the topic (aside from calls to make future pensions stingier, a different thing). What about the sorry state of municipal finance and education funding? No word. The escalating level of state debt? Nothing.

The "structural deficit" (what we call the deficit next year and after) gets a mention, and even some rhetorical flourishes. For example, the first page of the executive summary has a headline that reads "FY 2008 Budget Continues the Drive to Resolve the Structural Deficit." Unfortunately, the numbers from the budget's own executive summary (Figure 1.1, next page) show that the claim is utterly without merit. In other words, of the several biggest fiscal problems facing our state, this budget addresses none of them.

Structural deficit

The most extraordinary number in the FY08 budget is the estimate for the deficit *next* fiscal year: $379.2 million in 2009. The state is constitutionally required to balance its budget each year, but there's no requirement to balance it for the next year. We can often get through a year by selling some land, or finding some other source of one-time income, or by accounting changes. But the size of the next-year's deficit is a measurement of how honest we've been. A budget balanced honestly will have a low projected

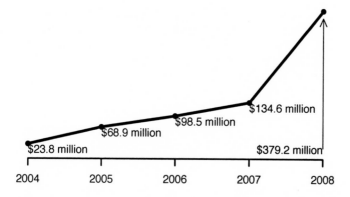

Figure 1.1: The "structural deficit." The graph above shows what Governor Carcieri's budget office thought the deficit would be the following year, in each of the budgets submitted since he took office. For the 2004 budget, this is the deficit that was anticipated for 2005. For FY08, it's the anticipated deficit in 2009. Each year has been worse than the year before, by a lot.

deficit the next year. What $379.2 million means is that our Governor is willingly and knowingly leading us to an even greater disaster than the one we're facing this year. Just for comparison, the next-fiscal-year deficit was $23 million in 2003, when the Governor oversaw the preparation of his first budget.

Clearly the Assembly bears a lot of responsibility for the situation. The Governor suggests a budget each year, and the Assembly passes a version of it that comports with its priorities. But the Governor owns these numbers. This is his own budget office's predictions of our fiscal situation in the next year, *if the budget is enacted as he suggests.* What we see is that for each year of his administration, the Governor has looked ahead, seen things getting worse than they are this year, and declined to act to stop them.

Betting the farm

There is another standout number in the future projections for the budget, and it's the projections of lottery revenue. (This includes both lottery ticket sales and revenue from the video terminals at Lincoln Park and Newport Grand.) News reports about the deficit have already said that lottery revenues are not up to last year's projections, but this isn't even half the story.

Figure 1.2 shows the lottery revenues, as presented in the budget documents for the last fiscal year, the present year and the next year. The first three points of each line are real data (though the third is only partial). The rest is just guesswork. Educated guesswork is what a budget *is*, so there's nothing wrong with that, but let's look closely at the three lines.

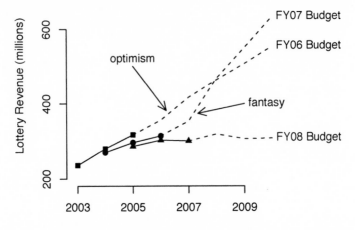

Figure 1.2: Lottery projections. The optimistic projections of the FY06 budget gave way to the incredibly optimistic projections of the FY07 budget despite the fact that collections were clearly leveling off. The projections used for the FY08 budget were more realistic, but by then, the damage was done.

As of 2005, when the 2006 budget was being put together, lottery revenues had been rising $25-30 million every year for the previous five years. Looking into what was then the future, budget forecasters apparently saw no reason that lottery revenue growth would decline, so they simply predicted that the growth would continue over the next five years. In the trade, this is called wildly optimistic, but it followed the trend, and had data to back it up, so is almost excusable.

In 2006, though, it was apparent that lottery revenues were leveling off. The 2005 revenues came in $11 million short of the predictions, and the growth in the previous three years was 18.9%, 9.4% and 5.7%. The trend was clearly *down*. So what did the budget office do? They predicted 12% growth in 2007 and *31%* growth in 2008. This is well past "wildly optimistic," and into the realm of outright delusional. In the figure, this line is marked "fantasy."

Trying to divine motives is the domain of mindreaders, not

data nerds, but it is reasonable to point out the number of ways in which these outrageous predictions served the needs of people in power. Most obviously, Governor Carcieri needed a balanced budget without lots of controversial cuts in order to be re-elected. He got it, and won re-election by a nose. After that, House Speaker Murphy was pushing a plan to cut the taxes of the wealthiest Rhode Islanders (the "flat" tax). Having a budget appear to be headed for deep deficit would not have helped enact a tax cut plan that will cost us tens of millions. He got what he needed, and the tax cut passed. Murphy's team may have also counted on the passage of the Narragansett Indian casino to shore up the lottery revenues, but they did not say so at the time.

As of 2007, it has become abundantly clear that the lottery revenue has leveled off, and the difference between the fantasies of last June and the reality of today is worth over half of our funding problem. Another way to look at this is that are were many people in the statehouse who knew last spring that we would be exactly where we are today.

Health care costs and benefits

All state departments are beset with escalating health care costs. But so are all the quasi-public agencies, so are all the cities and towns, and so are businesses and so are citizens. There are things we can do about this, but the Governor does not have them on his agenda. We have a Health Insurance Commissioner now, but he doesn't really have the legal tools to limit health care costs, only to limit health insurance costs, which is not the same thing.

There are reform ideas that have been sitting around for years that haven't gotten any traction under this Governor. For example, whatever you think about Beacon Mutual's governance, the fact is that they have become a very attractive Workers Compensation insurer for businesses in Rhode Island. Their rates are quite low compared to other companies, and their commitment is to Rhode Island. Why can't we reform escalating medical malpractice insurance rates the same way? For that matter, what about health insurance itself?

The Governor hangs his hopes on increasing competition. Yes, it is true that competition is low in Rhode Island, where there are really only two insurers of any note. But is competition a panacea? Statistics from the federal government show that you have to go

Table 1.1: Average premium for private-sector employees, and the average employee share of that cost. (Source: US Department of Health and Human Services, Agency for Healthcare Research and Quality, Medical Expenditure Panel Survey, 2004, tables VIII.C.1 and VIII.D.1. See www.meps.ahrq.gov/mepsweb.)

| | Family | | Single | |
	Premium	Employee	Premium	Employee
RI	10,220	2,309	4,368	794
CT	11,035	2,274	3,864	773
MA	10,559	2,784	4,141	885
NH	11,155	3,102	4,084	944
VT	10,690	2,657	4,074	744
ME	10,823	2,784	4,116	892
NY	10,397	2,090	3,882	714
NJ	11,425	1,885	3,858	613
PA	9,987	2,033	3,671	661
US	10,006	2,438	3,705	671

as far as Pennsylvania to find a state where family health insurance premiums are as low as they are here. (See Table 1.1. This is data from 2004.) Rhode Island premiums for single people, on the other hand, are as high as anywhere in the country. The other New England states have more health insurers than we do here, and so do New York and New Jersey. Many of them also have higher family premiums, so where is the evidence that competition alone will lower premiums? Could it be possible that we need competition for individual health plans, but not for family plans, or is it more likely that competition alone isn't going to do the trick?

The Governor's budget also contains $20 million to automate health care record-keeping. The idea is to establish a "Health Information Exchange" system (HIE) to make it easier for providers and insurers to share information, and therefore lower costs. But there seems to be no mechanism to make that second part of the equation happen. That is, it's fine to lower the costs of record-keeping to the hospitals, but exactly why should we pay for it from tax revenue without some way to insist—not just hope—that it will result in lower fees for care?

Education funding

The education aid section of the budget has a heading that reads: "Local Education Aid up $46.4 million Or 5..4 Percent." This is generously described as an exaggeration. In the matter of direct aid, the kind that goes to meeting a school department's bottom line, here's the way it splits up: all the schools that the state itself runs will see their budget allotments increased 6-10%, because that's how much their costs are going up. These are the state-run charter Met School (10.4%), Davies Vocational (7.0%), the School for the Deaf (5.7%), as well as the Central Falls school district (6.9%). For these schools, there isn't anyone to foist the expense onto, so the increase in costs must be shouldered by the state.

All the other school departments in the state are run by cities and towns, and they have taxpayers of their own. So they are scheduled to get only a 3% increase, and their property taxes will have to make up the difference. In other words, the numbers contain an admission that justifiable expenses are going up more than twice the 3% offered to local districts. It would cost about $23 million to bring the state's school districts up to the funding increase seen in Central Falls. The budget could hardly be clearer in indicating that increases in local property taxes are an essential part of it. Since the property tax is regressive, this is a bigger impact on the poor than on the wealthy. Since the legislature has lowered the limits on property tax increases to a level well below any of the increases seen by the state-run schools, this is only slightly less direct than simply telling school districts to cut programs.

State debt

There has been movement in the debt department, too. The state debt, after declining from $1.88 billion in 1994 to $1.28 billion in 2003, is now scheduled to go up to $2.13 billion in 2008. In other words, the debt reduction that took ten years, a lot of scrimping, and quite a bit of luck to achieve was undone in Governor Carcieri's first term, and state debt was up 66% in just five years. State revenue wasn't up nearly as fast, and the total debt is now 62% of revenue, up from 46% when the Governor took office. A debt of $2.1 billion costs around $243 million to service. In 2003, the total state debt cost only $122 million to service.

This accounting counts both tax-supported debt and the "GARVEE" bonds we've taken on to pay for relocating I-195, building a highway and rail line to Quonset and rebuilding the Sakonnet River Bridge and the Washington Bridge over the Seekonk River. These are supposed to be financed with federal highway money, and not supposed to count as "tax-supported." The budget was, however, fairly clear that the debt service for this debt was displacing other expenses, so the distinction seems a bit forced. For example, the Governor proposed that $67 million in one-time funds be spent on roads, largely because the federal highway money is already dedicated to these five massive projects, and smaller but equally important projects are languishing because of it.

These road projects aren't *bad* ideas, but is that true no matter what they cost?

Choosing a crisis

Rhode Island's fiscal crisis was chosen for us. This article is here as further proof. It contrasts our good economic position (as of 2005) with the fiscal problems of education, and is also included here because it tries to make concrete abstract terms like "progressive" and "regressive" taxes.

April 2005

A S IN MANY RECENT YEARS, schools across our state are in financial trouble this spring. Teachers, counselors and nurses are to be laid off in one town, neighborhood schools are to be closed in another, and most everything resembling a frill is pretty much history all over. Despite the cutting and slashing, however, property taxes to fund our schools (and municipal services) are higher than ever, and getting higher. Across the state, the same scenes are being played out in city council and school committee meetings, where the voices of reason insist that the only responsible thing is to slash spending, because there simply isn't any money to fund these nice things any more.

And yet, consider this. From 1991 to 2001, the US enjoyed one of the longest and most substantial economic expansions in modern history. The economy hasn't done as well since 2001, but even measured from 1991 to 2005, we're doing fine, averaging over 3% growth per year. Wages have been stagnant for a long time, and though they haven't kept up with inflation over the whole period, they made big gains in the late 1990s. Our nation's international trade position and the federal budget idiocy make for some very dark clouds on the economic horizon long-term, but in relative terms, what we've got on our hands right now isn't even a light drizzle, let alone an actual storm. Retail sales are up around 50% from 1990.[3] Rhode Island's unemployment rate is only slightly above the lowest it's been in 15 years, and declining. We have tens of thousands more jobs than we had 15 years ago, and around the same number of people. As the Governor's own budget has it, "Rhode Island's economic performance in 2004 has been nothing short of remarkable."[4] Why, then, are we having so much trouble paying for our children's education?

The conventional wisdom seems to be that the reason for this is exploding costs. In a sense, this is obviously the case: if the costs weren't rising, there wouldn't be a crisis. But simply knowing that costs are rising tells you precisely nothing about whether the increased spending is unjustifiable or unnecessary. Claiming otherwise without close examination is the mark of someone who isn't really interested in solving problems.

One issue is that we ask our schools to do more than we did even as recently as the 1980's. Two examples: special education has brought kids once deemed "ineducable" back into their communities, and state law now requires school systems to spend a great deal more on transportation than in the past. For most communities, these are both huge new expenses, leaving it somewhat less than a surprise that property taxes collected statewide have risen 33% since 1990. On average, you're paying a third more property tax than you did in 1990.[5].

But what may be a surprise to some is that during that same time, income tax collections have risen almost half again as fast: up 47%. What's more, over that same period, the effective state income tax *rate* has remained roughly constant or declined for most taxpayers, while property tax rates, um, haven't. And though this period includes the dramatic economic expansion of the 1990's, it also includes two recessions. We're collecting a lot more tax, but on average, you're paying state income tax at the same rate or significantly less than you did 15 years ago.

---

[3] All calculations are in constant 2005 dollars, unless otherwise noted.

[4] FY06 Budget, Executive summary, p.21, where you'll also find a more extensive discussion of how remarkable it is.

[5] And yes, this is true even if you rent. Few suspect that property taxes come out of a landlord's pocket, and that is part of our problem. See page 21

Tax fairness: a thought experiment

Let's imagine what would happen if taxes were raised in an essentially unfair way: arbitrary and overwhelmingly high, for many people, but low, on average. Say you have a sales tax that's only one percent for everyone whose last name starts with the letters A through U, and 50% for the poor unfortunates whose names bring up the rear of the alphabet.[6] On average, the tax would be around 4%, a bargain.

So this is hardly fair, not least because the burden has nothing to do with people's ability to pay, but how would the events actually play out? We'll assume that the tax would be eventually overturned, but what would happen on the way? Overall, the tax rate isn't huge, but people seldom make decisions based on aggregates. People make decisions about their own circumstances, and what they observe directly or hear about, and what many would see in our hypothetical case is that they would be paying much more tax than they could afford.

After a while those taxpayers would realize that there are many others in similar situations, and perhaps they would organize, to make their concerns more widely known. Having been told that the state constitution requires this kind of arrangement, perhaps their organizations would bring pressure to bear on local government to restrain spending, and perhaps they'd be able to enlist the aid of other people, who might not be as badly affected, but who can see the injustice of the situation. As government costs went up, increases in those taxes would have to be discussed. A 10% increase would bring the alphabetically challenged taxpayers' rates up to 55%, while the rest of us suffered under a 1.1% rate. I, of course, would have no problem with that, and might not bother showing up at hearings, but someone named Walsh would, and with his friends the Vennerbecks, Xaviers, Yorks and Zacharys, he'd be right to complain, loudly. But establishment policy shops could readily provide average statistics to "prove" that the tax burden is far from out of control. They'd say, but hey, the overall rate is still only 4.4%, and still a bargain.

The point of the example is that under an essentially unfair tax, rankling and outright rebellion will happen long before the average burden is unsustainable. It will look like complaints about

---

[6]This is about 6% of the population, according to the distribution of names of members of Congress.

spending, but it will happen *because* of the unfairness of the system, not the size of the load. Looking at who pays the tax is not just a detail; single numbers that are supposed to describe our tax system can be very misleading. The distinction between progressive and regressive taxes is not just academic. It has real consequences, and one of them is property tax riots. When discussing taxes, it's simply not good enough to look at what the overall level of tax is in the state. You have to look at where the burden falls, or you risk making idiotic tax policy decisions like this.

Tax policy in the real world

The actual tax policy decisions we've been living with over the past fifteen years haven't been so very different than this thought experiment. Motivated by some report from RIPEC or the Tax Foundation or the Heritage Foundation that ranks Rhode Island's tax burden in the top five or ten or whatever, our lawmakers repeatedly set out to raise no tax at all, and even to cut. If they succeed, it's usually by shifting the burden to the towns.[7] Some years the towns hold the line, and some years they can't. But all the pressure is from the state to the towns. There is no leverage in the other direction, and so the burden moves to the payers of the property tax, which is regressive (when it's not crazy).

Here's another thought experiment. For those who own houses: ask yourself and your friends, Could you afford the house you own, were it to come on the market today? For those who don't own their home, ask instead, Could you afford to move anywhere in the state that you'd actually choose to live? The answer, almost universally, is no—something all Rhode Islanders can share.

The real estate market is so crazy now, and has been so crazy for so long, that unless it was purchased quite recently, the value of one's home is very likely not at all a good measure of one's income. The officially assessed value, depending as it does on all kinds of assumptions and statistical artifacts, is likely even worse. The result is that you have people whose taxes bear little or no relation to their ability to pay, and are regularly subject to huge

---

[7] Or by not assuming what they'd planned to. Under Ed DiPrete, the stated goal of the administration was to move toward the point where the state picked up 60% of the statewide cost of education. Now it's hard to find legislators who think it could get back up to 40%. As of 2008, the number was about 32% according to numbers from the Department of Education, and may go below 30% in fiscal 2010.

swings during revaluation years. When these people show up to complain about property taxes at town council meetings, they are outraged, and it's usually justifiable. How can you blame someone who has just been told they can no longer afford to live in their own home?

Over the course of the past 15 years, municipal education costs have risen, but not faster than the growth of the economy, nor even faster than other parts of state government. But during that time, Rhode Island has allowed the increases in education costs to be assumed by the most arbitrary and least fair tax we have. Should we be surprised that tax revolts are a harbinger of spring around here?

What can we do to tame the crisis?

If you see the problem before us as an unsustainably high tax burden, as the Governor clearly does, there is only one responsible course of action: cut. Cut everything, cut desperately, and cut deep. But if you wonder why we can't seem to pay for what we can afford, perhaps looking for a solution that involves readjusting the distribution of the burden is a better idea. After all, the first involves cutting what doesn't really need cutting, and some of that stuff is valuable.

As was noted above, between 1990 and 2005, income tax collections have risen, despite two recessions. In 1997 Governor Lincoln Almond enacted a 10% income tax cut, phased in over five years. For many people in Rhode Island, the income tax is so low they didn't even notice, which is somewhat ironic, since politicans pass tax cuts in order to make themselves popular.

Repealing this cut would be useful, and raise about $100 million, and could keep important programs from being cut. But it would do little to address the overall fairness of the tax system. To do that requires shifting large amounts of revenue from one tax to another, for example, from the regressive property tax to the progressive income tax.

What would such a shift look like? Part of it would look like a tax increase, of course, but the other part would be the opposite. Suppose we raised the income tax 10% on everyone, and applied it all to property tax relief. This would allow a 7% property tax cut for everyone. Anyone whose state income tax bill is less than 93% of their property taxes would wind up with a net tax cut. Most people have to be earning well over $100,000 a year before they pay as much income tax as property tax, so this proposal would actually result in a net tax cut for around 95% of the state.

The logic works at more generous levels, as well. Were we to double the state income tax, and apply it to relief of property taxes, we could cut property taxes by 60%, have $200 million left over, and around 80% of the state would still be paying less in taxes. For the wealthy whose state taxes would increase, the change would be a bit smaller than the benefits of the Bush tax cuts they've received since 2001.

A little bit more detail. In North Kingstown, you are probably earning more than $99,000 before your income tax exceeds 60% of your property tax. In lower-tax Narragansett, the number is more like $77,000. In Providence, the number is nearer $122,000. Statewide, around 10% of filers claim more than $100,000 in income on their tax forms, and about 20% have income greater than $75,000.

There is a great deal that is appealing about a scenario like this, mainly that it would make our state's tax system more progressive, relieving much of the unfairness of the current system. But it's one thing to contemplate the perfect world, and it's entirely a different one to create it. There would be a host of knotty problems to untie.

One of the most significant obstacles is landlords. How do you get the tax relief past them and to the people for whom it's intended? Counting on landlords to lower the rent is probably not a good strategy. A rental tax credit is one way to do it, though there would be a certain amount of overhead to manage it. This is a hard problem, but rather than take it as discouragement, let it illustrate a more important point: it's much harder to undo bad policy than it is to keep from making it in the first place. Acting may be hard, but not acting can be worse.

Another problem is that some towns benefit a great deal from the property tax. These are the seaside towns with lots of out-of-state landowners. The multimillion-dollar beach homes in Narragansett are what allow the taxes to remain low on the rest of the town. These towns might find it best to provide property tax relief via renters-and-homesteaders exemptions on people who actually live in town, in order to preserve the income from their out-of-towners.

Yet another potential obstacle was outlined by a town councillor I spoke to recently. He said that it sounded interesting, but you had to look at the whole context, and cautioned me that CVS's Tom Ryan might flee the state, taking his zillion-dollar income with him. Concern about the unintended consequences of policy is important, but paralysis is also a problem. Rich people might flee, and they might not. One can't know in advance, and one certainly can't find out by asking. But it is not true that action is less responsible or more risky than inaction. They both constitute a choice: one chooses to try a solution, and the other chooses not to. This caution is the false "responsibility" of those who would watch the house burn rather than risk the water damage. We have a lot of these people around, though, and they will be (and have been) a serious obstacle to change.

City/state trust

Towering over these cavils, however, is the real obstacle, the one that has, until now, prevented our government from addressing the inequities of the state's various tax laws: trust. The Governor and state legislators don't seem to trust the towns with increases in money and the towns don't trust that the state will pay what it promises. (And our city councils don't really trust their school committees, either.) Until the fundamental relation between the state and the towns is repaired, reform will be elusive.

The obstacles to this kind of reform are many, but the goal is well worth it. Fixing the way we fund education is the Gordian knot of Rhode Island policy: hard to unravel, but well worth taking the time to try. At least things worked out pretty well for the last guy who managed to untie one.

Difficult is not the same as impossible. One way to manage the trick is to get courts involved. Back in the early 1990's, after a court ruling unfavorable to the current method of funding education, much talk was heard about a Guaranteed Student Entitlement. This was to be an amount of money that each student in every town would be guaranteed for their education, and was to be written to become an enforceable compact between towns and the state. Because no politician at the time was willing to suggest the tax changes necessary to fund such an entitlement fairly, and few towns were willing to submit to the budgetary scrutiny such a proposal entailed, the whole project faded to obscurity. But its failure had more to do with a lack of political courage than with the merits of the idea.

I'm with Tolstoy: saying that we as a populace "choose" this or that is a convenient, but terribly misleading metaphor. "We" didn't choose to have a crisis in school funding. But it was choices, made and followed by popular Governors (and legislators, though they're less popular), that have caused this crisis. It is a crisis by choice.

So how did these choices cause a school funding crisis? By creating a fundamentally regressive tax structure. How do we fix it? By making the tax code more progressive. Admittedly, this answer contradicts the conventional wisdom about government spending and the tax burden, but if the conventional wisdom were always correct, wouldn't we be living in an earthly paradise?

The problem with entitlements

Why is cutting the budget so hard? Is it because the legislature is stupid and corrupt, or is it because the budget is more complicated than most people think?

February 2008

IT SEEMS, SOMETIMES, that everyone knows what the problem is with the state budget. From the Governor to members of the Assembly, and from radio talkers to friends and neighbors, I hear people claiming that we have to rein in "entitlements."

When I talk to people about this, they often reason like this: there aren't any prominent politicians defending entitlement spending. But yet it seldom gets cut by appreciable amounts. Therefore, there must be a powerful poverty lobby in whose iron grip the legislature can only squirm helplessly. Alternate versions of the conventional tale have it that the legislature is riddled with malevolent union stooges all too willing to stick it to the beleaguered taxpayer in favor of defending their privileges.

But this is silly. The staffs of the groups devoted to lobbying on behalf of the poor are small, distinguished mainly by a willingness to accept low pay and crazy hours. In recent years, despite winning a few skirmishes here and there, they have lost a lot of ground. Rhode Island has stingy welfare benefits, and they're stingier than they were twelve years ago, just like other states. And there are, indeed, union members of the legislature, but they apparently couldn't stop the pension reform legislation of a couple of years ago, nor the school aid cuts of last year, so as a conspiracy, they're not very effective.

But if it's not a spectacularly effective lobby or a powerful infiltrators, why, then, do people keep complaining about entitlements? Why doesn't the Governor just cut them all?

There is, of course, a third possibility: cutting "entitlements" is harder than you think it is, because "entitlements" are probably not what you think they are.

In this year's budget documents, there's a pie chart up front that shows that "Assistance, Grants, and Benefits" make up 41% of all state spending. That's $2.8 billion out of a total budget only a hair below $7 billion. Shocking, isn't it? This contains welfare, RIte Care, child care benefits and all the rest. But what you may not realize is this is just an accounting category covering expenses incurred by nearly every state department. Did you know it also contains tuition aid at the state colleges, temporary disability insurance (TDI) payments and unemployment insurance (UI) checks? Not to mention the money we pay the Rhode Island Historical Society to take care of the state's collection of battle flags and the Gorham silver service made to use on the U.S.S. Rhode Island.

What's more, almost half this category—$1.24 billion—is federal funds. About a billion is state tax money, and $587 million is restricted money that can only be spent on a specific purpose, like UI and TDI premiums.

Welfare, cash payments to poor families with children, makes up only a tiny fraction of this money: about $55 million, less than 1% of total state budget. The "exploding" cost of child care benefits is around $50 million. For the two programs together, we receive about $80 million in federal funds. You do the math and tell me whether this is what's breaking our bank.

So what *is* this money? Mostly Medicaid, at $1.7 billion. Less than half of that is state tax dollars, but $833 million isn't loose change. Still, less than a third of Medicaid is health insurance for poor people, how many people think of it. The rest is payments to hospitals for people who don't have insurance, payments to nursing homes for disabled and elderly people, support services for the developmentally disabled and so on. The Governor is proposing to address this spending in some positive ways, and that's a good thing, but without turning elderly nursing home residents out of doors, it's hard to see how we get the dollar savings he proposes as quickly as he hopes.

So what about cutting people from RIte Care? That's $500 million, or, well, $238 million in state funds. Yes, but did you notice that part in the previous paragraph about "payments to hospitals for people who don't have insurance." When fewer poor people have health insurance, we'll be paying more to the hospitals. Plus, every dollar of state funds cut means $2.12 cut from the state's economy as we give up the federal match.

See? It's complicated. You don't need to believe that our legislature is run by a pack of thieves to see why it's so hard to cut entitlement spending. But you need to understand the issues facing the government we actually have, instead of just railing against the government you imagine we have.

Incidentally, none of this is to say that there aren't lots of places where a sane government would spend less money. Here's one: The state employs over 160 "Eligibility Technicians" whose only job is to help people who need welfare assistance to fill out the forms and figure out which programs they qualify for. Our welfare laws are such a welter of confusing regulations that few people can fill out the many forms on their own. I know I couldn't.

We could make this simpler, but it would require time to figure out how to resolve conflicting regulations and effort to reprogram the computers and make new forms. Which is to say that dealing with this issue would require capacity that the Department of Human Services simply doesn't have. After years of cutbacks, DHS is barely able to fulfill its core functions, let alone plan improvements—even the ones that save money. Real application reform (and have you ever heard so banal a call for reform?) would save a bundle, and make the program far more efficient, but it will cost money up front, so can never happen in an environment where every penny has to be squeezed out right now.

Why are banks in charge?

While the economy won't run without banks, we shouldn't let banks run the economy. Here are just a few reasons why.

May 2009

WHY IS IT A BAD IDEA to let banks run our economy? In April 2009, we saw evidence. First bank lobbyists successfully killed the "cramdown" provisions of the bankruptcy reform legislation in the Senate. Cramdown is an unmusical term for allowing a bankruptcy judge to modify the terms of a home mortgage. You may not be aware that a judge can modify the terms of a loan for a business or a vacation home or a yacht, but not a primary home. Foreclosures and bankruptcies litter our economic playing field, so it makes some sense to reduce these.

Not to the banks. Bank lobbyists (with the laudable exception of Citigroup's) insisted that the "moral hazard" was too great, and that people would be going bankrupt willy-nilly if this passed, to get their mortgage terms changed. This, of course, is both inane and hypocritical, too. Inane because going into bankruptcy is hardly the kind of thing anyone does lightly. Hypocritical because the bank lobby's position on issues of their own moral hazard (i.e. unaccountable executive pay) is that it's simply not a problem, even though the evening news continues to scream otherwise.

But no matter. As Sen. Dick Durbin (D-Il) said about his Senate colleagues, "Banks own this place." Rhode Island's Senators Jack Reed and Sheldon Whitehouse voted right, but only 43 other Democrats did, and so the measure went down to defeat. So that wave of foreclosures will continue to wash over us.

On the very same day, a few hedge funds and investment banks forced Chrysler into bankruptcy by refusing to settle their claims to the company's assets. This is altogether too bloodless a way to describe it. More accurately, several thousand people will be put out of work because a few millionaires refused to voluntarily sacrifice anything at all on their behalf.

But what about the Gordon Gekko "greed is good" perspective on the economy? The idea was Adam Smith's: that if we all look out for #1, then everything works out best for everyone. It's a dandy theory, but I don't see it corroborated by the facts on the ground. What I see is a great deal of angst and suffering caused by a few people who appear to feel zero responsibility to the very society that made them fabulously wealthy individuals.

Back here in Rhode Island, we've gone out of our way to make life good for banks and bankers—cutting taxes, lifting usury laws and even offering sweetheart mortgages to bank presidents[8]—but the real impact on the conduct of state business has been in the financialization of policy.

Take the continuing strife over state employee pensions. The unfunded liability of the pension system is large and that's a problem. But the bottom line for any pension system is only that the pension checks don't bounce. All the rest is detail about what's the least painful way to do that, and there is more than one way. One strategy is that we accumulate money in a pension fund, invest it and pay the pensions out of the proceeds.

That should sound familiar, since it's the traditional way. But there's another way. We could invest the money in our citizens—improving child welfare, public schools and higher education—and pay the pensions out of tax collections levied from a state economy grown as a result of these investments. This might not sound familiar, but paying increased expenses with economic growth is how Social Security has worked for decades. Even without the income from its trust fund, Social Security taxes will be adequate to cover its pensions for years to come.

So those are two different ways to pay employee pensions in decades to come. But only one is ever considered, and the reason is that Rhode Island policy makers rely only on the banker's view of what constitutes investment. To them, buying stock in Lehman Brothers, or a 30-year bond from General Motors is investment, while spending money to improve a child's education is only expense. And don't tell me about risk, please. As we're seeing, the safest public investments are likely *not* financial. The economies best positioned to weather this economic storm are the very places that have the best-educated populaces: Massachusetts, for example, but also Germany, France and Finland.

The financialization of policy extends much further. Rather than carry a fund balance from which to pay our bills, the state and lots of cities and towns rely on short-term borrowing ("tax anticipation notes"). This is not a problem so long as interest rates

---

[8]Fleet Bank CEO Terry Murray got one from a RI Housing program for low-income home buyers in the 1980's.

are low, but disaster looms when they aren't. It's not free, either.
The price of keeping a low fund balance is millions of tax dollars spent on commissions to bond traders, in addition to the debt
service.

There's more. Rather than raise the revenue for investment
in our universities, we cover the lack by borrowing in order to
build fancy buildings that won't be filled because of staffing cuts.
Rather than raise the revenue for road maintenance, we borrow
outrageously in order to replace rusty bridges in Providence and
on the Sakonnet River.

All this means we have a colossal state debt—almost twice as
big as when Governor Carcieri arrived—so we desperately need
to stay in the good graces of the bankers to keep our interest rate
low. So we do what they say when they tell us to keep a "rainy day
fund" or to pay pensions in a specific way, or to cut the budget.

Here's the important part. From a banker's perspective it all
makes perfect sense. If money is what you own, unemployment is
not nearly as threatening as inflation. Keeping workers employed
at Chrysler, letting people ease their mortgage payments, investments in education and road maintenance all have stimulative effects on the economy, and stimulation can lead to inflation and
inflation is a banker's worst enemy.

Me, I have more labor than money, so I fear unemployment—a
reduced demand for labor—much more than inflation. The people who share my situation vastly outnumber those who don't, so
I continue to wonder why it is that big bankers call so many of
the shots.

Two

A Closer Look

The roads ahead

If you had to choose a single department to blame above the others for our fiscal crisis, it would be hard not to choose the Department of Transportation. The borrowing practices in that department beggar belief, and yet we have come to think of them as routine ways to do the public's business. I've left the tenses alone in this piece, so it can be used again in 2010.

September 2008

THE PRIMARY IS BEHIND US and the election looms. In November 2008, you'll see a Rhode Island tradition on the ballot: the Transportation bond. Every two years, since at least the DiPrete administration, Rhode Islanders are asked to approve another huge round of bonds for roads. Ho hum, isn't that how people build roads?

Well no. Virtually no other states fund their roads this way. Sure, lots of states borrow for a specific highway here or a bridge there. But we borrow for no specific project, an astonishingly wasteful practice.

At this point, DOT borrows about $40 million a year, no matter what. We use that money to match federal dollars awarded on the proviso that the state come up with a 10% or 20% match to the funds. We spend the sum on whatever projects are at the top of the "to-do" list that year.

Now there are a couple of legitimate reasons for borrowing. You might want to amortize some expense over several years, like when you buy a house. Or you might expect the investment to have a payoff down the road, as with student loans or business investments. But neither of these apply to our roads. That is, our expenses are *already* amortized—at $40 million per year—and none of the road projects on tap involve expanding our transportation capacity. Mostly they involve repairing or replacing what we've already got.

But we can't ignore an important illegitimate reason for borrowing: to hide the true cost of the government people demand. Compared to many other government services, roads and bridges are popular, if expensive. Cars need them, people demand them, and, oh boy, have we built them. We've almost doubled the length of our road system since 1950 and far more than doubled the capacity with lots of big expensive highways.[1]

From what I can tell from old budget documents and DOT reports, the borrowing habit probably began with the construction of the interstate highways. These were good candidates for funding with debt. They were ambitious undertakings that made a tremendous difference in transportation (good and bad). And they also brought rivers of federal cash flowing down the corridors of the state house.

When those projects were completed in the mid-1970's, the torrent of federal money threatened to turn into a trickle, so apparently budget writers at the statehouse decided to keep on borrowing to keep the federal funds flowing. You can see this in the size and frequency of the bond issues. The Garrahy years were tentative, with a few small bond issues, a couple of which were even voted down, but under Ed DiPrete, we started borrowing serious money.

And what a mess we've made with it. Until quite recently, the feds wouldn't pay for maintenance, only new construction and improvements. So we found excuses to rebuild where only maintenance was required. We widened and straightened country roads that only needed repaving, put up pointless street lights, and found excuses to replace bridges that only needed repairs. All to keep that river of cash flowing.

The new roads not only made big profits for construction companies, but also for a large number of people who owned suburban land. Land developers, mall owners, farmers who sold off a piece of their fields and many more have cashed in since the early 1980's. Land development was a good substitute for industry. Who'd want to spoil that party by putting a price tag on it?

---

[1] For more about our expanding network of roads and bridges, see "Where did the money go?" on page 81.

Certainly not Ed DiPrete, Lincoln Almond or Don Carcieri. (Bruce Sundlun wasn't suburban, and he cut the borrowing.)

By now, the imperative to keep the Federal River flowing at little cost has made a fiscal disaster. The debt has piled higher every year, and we've used serpentine contortions to avoid dealing with it. For example, when debt service threatened to bring the DOT budget into the red in the 90's, an employee-free Department of Debt Service Payments was created to move these payments to a different page of the budget.[2] At $41 million this year, DOT has far and away the biggest chunk of that department.

Combining debt service paid from within the department's budget, we now pay almost $100 million every year in DOT *debt service*.[3] How does that make you feel about borrowing $40 million more next year? Do you think that's a sensible way to run the state?

Shuffling debt around wasn't even the worst of it. In the early 1990's, it became clear that DOT was paying its employee salaries with borrowed money. Lincoln Almond directed the agency to put an end to that, but didn't allocate any more money with which to do so. The agency cut its staff by over 100 employees, but its use of contracted services nearly doubled. Contracted services can be allocated to specific construction projects, so can be paid with federal funds, and so between 10% and 20% of those services is paid with borrowed money.

In 2007, it came to light that DOT was paying $102,000 to a contractor for the services of a typist who earned $38,000. This is scandalous, certainly, but the real outrage is that the reason this woman was a contractor and not a state employee is so that her salary could be paid with federal money—and the borrowed state match. We hear about contracting services as a way to save money, but paying this woman $38,000 in 2007 cost the state over $120,000 once you count the debt service for her salary. It's hard to see how that saves us any money.

---

[2] It's still there, between the Office of Energy Resources and Security Services.

[3] This counts debt incurred by the so-called "GARVEE" bonds. These bonds are meant to be repaid not by taxes, but by future federal highway dollars. A somewhat smaller debt will be repaid by gas taxes diverted to the Economic Development Corporation before they reach the state's general revenue. Of course the construction and repairs those dollars won't pay for will be paid for by other taxes, so the distinction is absurd on its face. Nonetheless, legal technicians in the statehouse deemed it to be distinction enough to allow the state to take on $700 million in new debt without a referendum.

The worst part of the borrowing story is the cynical packaging of the bond referenda. This year's bond is worth $80 million in DOT borrowing (for the two years until the next election), but on the ballot you'll also see $3.5 million each for RIPTA and for a commuter rail station in North Kingstown. Why are these on the same ballot question? When DEM has two or three different projects to fund, they appear in two or three different ballot questions. These transportation projects (whose proceeds don't even go to the same agency) are put together only because the budget writers calculate that the odds of passage are higher if they include a pittance for public transit with the DOT lard.

How did we get to this pass? Simple: we allowed politicians to pretend they were managing our finances in a responsible fashion while they borrowed way past any reason to spend freely on expensive roads and bridges, all the while pinching pennies on the public transit that could save us all money and time. I'm tired of these games, and intend to vote no on the transportation bond this November. Please join me.

The truth about unfunded liabilities

The state's pension system plays a big part in discussions of the state budget. What many people don't realize is that its high cost stems from an attempt to be more fiscally responsible than anyone requires us to be. This foolish policy is where much of the real expense of the system lies.

March 2009

SOMETIME IN THE FUTURE, a storm might come and knock down your house. If it does, rebuilding will cost a lot of money. Suppose you could shore up your house now, with a stronger roof and steel beams, but it would cost so much you'll have to sell all your furniture to afford it. Would you prevent a disaster in the future by voluntarily undergoing one today?

The people managing the state's pension system say yes. Public employee pensions are on a lot of people's minds. There's a legislative commission looking into them, and some alarming testimony came from the Treasurer's office last week about the rising cost of pensions, which provoked predictable calls for slashing them, again.

You'll hear people say that the system we use to pay the pensions of teachers and state employees is short $5 billion and that sounds terrible. It's not great, that's for sure, but it's worth being sure you understand the real problem. An "unfunded liability" like this means that the pension system would need $5 billion more in order to pay pensions from the investment income of the fund. That's a little less than is in the fund already. Whatever pension costs aren't covered by the investment income have to be covered by tax revenue.

There's a difference between a public and a private pension system that is crucial to understand. The motivation for wanting your system to be fully funded is very different. As we're seeing, even companies as big as General Motors can get in trouble and some of them even disappear. In order to keep the promises to their employees, private pension systems have to be 100% funded, with no unfunded liability, so they can pay benefits even if the company vanishes. So there are laws that require full funding for private companies.

But a state isn't going to go out of business. A public pension system wants to keep the funding level high, but for a wholly different set of reasons. Investment income varies from year to year, and the needs of retirees varies, too. A system funded at 90% will be easier to budget for than a system at our 55%, because the amount necessary to make up the difference won't vary as much. The state that runs a fully funded system will find that system easier to budget for than a state whose system is less well funded.

What's important to understand, though, is that in neither case are the retirees in danger of not getting checks. It's less of a burden on the government in one case, but that's the only difference. Until the reform of 1986, Social Security, for example, happily paid its benefits at what amounted to about a 10% funding level. That's 50 years without trouble, and it's not entirely clear to many whether the reform helped matters.

Back to the state pension system. Where did our unfunded liability come from? It came from three years of missed payments in the 1990's, from decades of sweetheart pension deals to legislators and other insiders (awards of pension "credit" for people who didn't pay into the system), and from some bad guesses our actuaries made. It didn't come from the employees themselves, who pay 8.75% of their salaries (9.5% for teachers) into the system, a much higher level than most systems require. The pensions are good, but they are paid for.

In 1999, the legislature decided to do something about the unfunded liability, and started us down a 30-year course to pay it off. Our actuaries report that in 2030, the payments will go down by a factor of twenty. That's worth working towards, but unfortunately, right after we set about that course, the stock market tanked. Paying off the liability by 2029 suddenly became a lot harder. Undaunted by reality, the decision-makers forged ahead, determined to be fiscally responsible by not contemplating putting off the magic date a couple of years. Because of this, the vast bulk of state and local pension payments is for paying off the liability, not for paying checks to retirees this year.

Now we're in the middle of a crisis, and it's not just a crisis in the investment markets. That is, along with the crisis in the investment markets, our actuaries estimate that the wave of retirements of September, 2008, will cost the system at least $33 million. Plus, an unexpected drop of almost 1200 employees paying in to the system means that $20 million has to be found somewhere. (For some perspective, usually around 1200 people retire from state and school service in any given year.) The actuaries' report says these retirements will save the state $100 million in payroll costs, but we pay for that in reduced services *and* increased pension costs.

The goal of the pension "reform" proponents is to reduce the unfunded liability, by reducing the pensions. Aside from the problem of accidentally provoking another rush to the exits, there is a fairness issue. The employees we're talking about didn't create the unfunded liability, legislators, governors and actuaries did.

But really, it's slightly beside the point. It's a good thing to pay off the unfunded liability, but there's nothing magical about the year 2029. What's the matter with 2039? We could cut the pension payments by 15% simply by delaying the payoff a few years. To be clear, that's almost $60 million, shared between the state and school departments.

This might sound like giving in, or being fiscally imprudent, but tell it to the radicals in North Dakota, Iowa, or Kentucky, whose pension systems refinance the unfunded liability *every year*. This is far from unusual in pension systems, and it's called an "open" amortization schedule. The progress toward paying off the liability isn't as quick, but it isn't nothing either. Fiscal responsibility is good, but since when is it fiscally responsible to break the bank in the name of fiscal responsibility?

It's a fine thing not to burden our children with huge pension payments, but our children are currently in schools suffering from the huge increase in pension payments, so it's not like there's an obvious benefit to them. Like the owner of that storm-plagued house, we're suffering now from the very problem this policy is supposed to prevent. Does that make sense?

It's a crime

Where has the money gone? Much of it has gone to expensive policy choices we've made, a fact that's often ignored. Along with crime fighting choices, outlined here, Chapter 5 describes some others.

October 2007

AS THE STATE CONTINUES TO WRESTLE with its budget crisis, you hear a lot about unions and pensions and state employees. What you seldom hear about is the expensive policy choices we've made. Welfare reform, for example, may or may not have been a good idea, but why anyone thought that providing child care, job training and transition health insurance would be cheap remains a mystery. We've opened a lovely new bridge in Providence, but let's remember that this $700 million project was originally proposed as a substitute for $50 million in bridge repairs. And now let's talk about getting tough on crime.

In 1988, our state's jails housed 1,528 people. As of September, there were 3,937. In 1988 we spent $47 million on them. This year, we're expecting to spend $199 million. In 1988 we had just over 10,000 people on probation or parole, and now there are almost 27,000. In other words, after accounting for inflation, we're spending about 2.6 times as much now as in 1988, taking care of 2.6 times as many prisoners and monitoring 2.7 times as many probationers. Per prisoner, we're spending about the same now as we did then. The trouble is only there are many more prisoners now.

1988 was notable because that year the Assembly passed legislation establishing a mandatory minimum sentence of 10 years for people convicted of possession of as little as one ounce of heroin or cocaine. We also amended the state constitution to deny bail for drug offenses where the potential sentence was 10 years or more. Sounds tough, right? These measures were put in place to be tough on crime, but whether you think them effective or draconian, they cost a lot. In the very first year, the number of female inmates jumped from 87 in 1988 to 215 in 1989.[4]

One of the more troubling things about our expensive policy choices is that frequently there is no one who chose them. For example, during the 1990's, there was a substantial drop in crime across America. Why this happened is the source of a great deal of argument, with many people claiming that their approach was the silver bullet. Steven Levitt, the economist who wrote *Freakonomics* (with Stephen Dubner, 2005), has spent some time with crime statistics, trying to answer this question. In a 2004 paper,[5] he suggested that the most easily identifiable causes were the increases in police and the increases in prisons, but that increasing police has a bigger effect for a smaller amount of money.

With that in mind, let's review the record in Rhode Island. Over the past several years, we've added police officers in exactly the places where they're least needed, while the places where we need them, we've barely kept even, or lost officers. Which is to say that our state is spending more on its police now than in 2000, but they're all in places like Charlestown and Little Compton, not in Pawtucket and Woonsocket, where the police forces have been cut.

Who is responsible for this brilliant crime-fighting strategy? Pretty much no one. Charlestown can add a police officer because Charlestown is growing fast enough to pay for him or her, and

---

[4]In 2007 and again in 2008, the legislature voted to repeal the mandatory minimums, but Governor Carcieri vetoed the repeal so they remain on the books. The Assembly leadership has refused to schedule veto override votes, despite the bill having passed with veto-proof majorities.

[5]"Understanding why crime fell in the 1990s: Four factors that explain the decline and six that do not," *Journal of Economic Perspectives*, 18(1), 2004, pp163–190. Notoriously, he also found that a highly significant factor was the advent of legal abortion in the US a generation before.

that's pretty much that. But about an eighth of Charlestown's non-education budget comes from the state, so their spending choices do have an impact on everyone else.

For the sake of analysis, I somewhat arbitrarily put the towns into three groups: towns that grew less than 1% between 2000 and 2005, towns that grew between 1% and 2.5%, and towns that grew more than 2.5%. For perspective, the statewide population growth between 2000 and 2005 was 1.35%.

The high-growth list was dominated by the towns of South County, but also included Lincoln, Foster and Glocester, a pretty rural list. These towns increased the size of their police payrolls by 16.25% between 2000 and 2006, though their population only grew by 4.1%.

The medium-growth cohort was harder to characterize. It had some cities (Providence and Central Falls), some first-ring suburbs (Cranston, Johnston), some second-ring suburbs (East Greenwich, North Kingstown) and some rural towns (Little Compton, Burrillville). These towns increased the size of their populations by 1.8% between 2000 and 2005, and grew their police departments' payrolls by 5.1%, on average.

With the exception of Barrington and North Smithfield, the low-growth places are a fairly urban group. They included Woonsocket, Newport, East Providence, and Pawtucket, among others. This group actually lost 2.17% of its police payroll, while its population barely moved. And what a surprise. Most of the high-crime towns are in the low-growth group and most of the low-crime towns are in the high-growth group. Police are not hired where they're most needed, but where towns can afford them.

The summary is this: we have spent and continue to spend a lot on prisons largely because we enacted drug laws that fill them up. There are plenty of ways to control crime for less expense. We could invest in drug treatment programs, we could end mandatory minimum sentences, we could reform our parole system,[6] we could hire more police officers. Instead, we rely on the most expensive possible crime-fighting strategy: lots of prisons, fewer police. We do manage to spend money on police, but by leaving all such decisions under local control, we guarantee that the police

---

[6]Parole revocation hearings have a much lower standard of evidence than trials. We have several prisoners who are in jail because their parole was revoked for offenses of which they were later found innocent.

hired won't be in the communities where they could do the most
good. No one has decided to do things so badly, and yet here we
are, doing them badly. Now tell me again why there's a budget
crisis?

The fun only lasts until the music stops

*It's quite common to hear legislators and suburban politicians tsk-
ing at the fiscal plight of our cities. But the evidence that these folks
have been any more responsible about their budget is completely
superficial, and doesn't survive much scrutiny.*

May 2009

IN MAY 2009, during a hearing at the Senate Finance committee,
chairman Daniel DaPonte (Democrat of East Providence and
Pawtucket) made some disparaging remarks about our cities and
towns. In response to a witness who made a comment about how
cuts in municipal aid are forcing cities and towns to raise property taxes, Senator DaPonte said, "There is no evidence that giving cities and towns more money will result in property tax cuts.
We've raised municipal aid a lot and property taxes haven't come
down."

The chairman is right and wrong. He's right that municipal
aid has gone up a lot—from $28 million in 1990 to $234 million in
2008. What are the towns doing with all that money? Flushing it
down the toilets in town hall?

In fact, they can't flush it because they don't get even half of it.
That number serves to nurse the conventional tale about what's
wrong with government around here, but it doesn't have much to
do with paying the bills at town hall. You see, to make the sum as
large as $234 million, the state budget writers include $135 million
in reimbursement for car taxes. This is real money, certainly, and
it's *related* to municipal budgets, but it goes to taxpayers, not to
municipalities. It does not help balance those budgets

In a way, the car tax reimbursements perfectly encapsulate the
dominant attitude towards towns up on Smith Hill: we think property taxes are too high, but we don't trust the cities and towns to

do anything about it. So we'll give them some money, but only if they give it to their taxpayers, not to your employees. Everyone agrees that municipal budgets are under a lot of pressure, but how this really helps them isn't clear.

If you ignore the car tax reimbursements, state aid to cities and towns is down, pretty much any way you slice it, as a proportion of state spending, as a proportion of municipal budgets and as a proportion of the state's economy.

The year 1990 was probably the high-water mark for municipalities at the state house. For all his faults, Ed DiPrete was a former mayor, and therefore was the last governor we've had who had ever spent time balancing a local budget. It's no surprise that under his administration, the stated policy of the state was to work towards funding 60% of local education costs. At the time, state aid was funding 31% of total municipal budgets, not counting federal grants, and about 42% of school budgets.

But the 1991-92 fiscal crisis knocked everyone for a loop, and Bruce Sundlun was a lot of things, but mayor was never one of them. State aid fell to 23% of municipal budgets. Lincoln Almond's administration slowly pushed it back up to 33%, but it's been declining ever since Governor Carcieri took over, and we're down to 27% as of 2008 (including only 36% of education costs, counting generously). It's a little hard to say what's the case in 2009, since the dust hasn't settled, but the only real question is how great the decline.

For cities and towns, what's the difference between Lincoln Almond (33%) and Don Carcieri (27%)? About $160 million in local aid, that's what. But you'd rather have a couple of replacement bridges, wouldn't you?

Wait a minute, you say. Even though municipal aid is down so much, you're measuring it in relation to other numbers that have also gone up. What about the real number?

Fair enough. As of 1990, Rhode Island cities and towns received about $1.3 billion, between state aid and property taxes. In 2008, the comparable number was a bit short of $3 billion. If you're keeping score, that's growth of about 1.9% per year after correcting for inflation. This is troubling, but it's not necessarily evidence of mismanagement. Inflation measures the price of goods and a few services, while towns spend their money on services and a few goods. The CPI may not be the best measure here.

If you want a useful yardstick with which to measure a service-oriented enterprise like a city or a town, how about Federal Express? That company is widely thought of as a fierce competitor that relies on technology to keep costs down, and only a few of its employees, like its pilots, belong to a union. How do they do? Well, in 1990, it cost $11 to send an overnight letter to California, and today it's about $25.50 for the same service. After correcting for inflation, that's up about 2% a year. Health care is also a service industry, and I think we'd all be much happier if it had kept its costs down to 2% growth. On the other hand, movie ticket prices are actually down compared to inflation, so not all service industries see cost inflation.

What about the state? After accounting for inflation in the same way, the state's general revenue has gone up 2.4% per year since 1990, and overall expenses are up even more.

This is what makes it so galling to sit around in town hall these days. Here you are, running your town more efficiently than Fedex, and *way* more efficiently than the state, but look how you're treated.

I'm not saying 1.9% a year is great. My income hasn't gone up that fast. It's a cause for concern for me, and should be for you, too. I'm not counseling complacency; government needs watchdogs. But we're not going to fix anything by getting all the important answers wrong. In this case, putting the blame on the cities and towns tends to absolve the state, which by comparison has been downright reckless with its finances at the same time it starves the cities and towns.

We have nearly doubled the state debt since 2002, for example, taking on giant road projects we can't afford. We have stolen from the following fiscal year in service of the current year. And we've given millions of tax dollars to the wealthiest of our citizens, tax cuts the state's budget-writers still haven't given up on, even despite the crisis.

The big difference between the state and the municipalities here is the state's tax revenue grows in step with the economy, while towns have to raise tax rates in order to keep up. Towns pay for their tax increases in the form of property tax riots, while the state gets its increases for free, as it were. For years, all those cost-of-living adjustments and allowances for the rising price of fuel are built into the state's funding source, so they're easy to build into the budgets. Except for the fastest-growing towns, this was a pleasure denied to municipalities. Legislators and the Governor can tsk the way they do at the locals because the state has been insulated from their budgetary recklessness by this constantly growing stream of income.

Until, of course, the music stops. This year, collections from the state income and sales taxes have declined, and the state is reeling from accumulated years of irresponsible budgeting, and naturally, the state is blaming cities and towns again. Some things never change.

Three

Economical Advice

Our economic woes: Doing it to ourselves

During the annual debates about taxes and the cost of government, it's easy to forget that economic reasoning supports a progressive system of taxation at least as well as the argument from fairness. Some of the best evidence comes from the radicals at Moody's Investor Services and economy.com.

March 2009

THE ESSENCE OF GREEK TRAGEDY is that the hero does it to himself. King Creon destroys his family through his stubborn insistence on punishing Antigone. Oedipus was, well, blind to his own quick temper, and if he hadn't killed that guy he met on the road, things might have turned out differently for him.

At this point, it's hard to argue that Rhode Island's fiscal problems are not self-inflicted. Yes, we're in an economic crisis, but the state's books were way out of balance even in 2006 when the economy was still booming, and we blindly cut taxes to make it all worse.

But what a lot of people don't appreciate is how much of our economic problems are self-inflicted. Some interesting evidence comes from data developed to determine how best to stimulate our economy.

In the summer of 2008, Mark Zandi, of economy.com (the economic consultant the state uses), presented to the US Congress some estimates of the efficacy of different kinds of government spending. He calculated that a dollar of spending on an across-the-board tax cut would net $1.03 in benefit to the nation's economy. A dollar cut from corporate taxes would net about 30 cents of

42

benefit, while a dollar of extended unemployment benefits would net $1.64.

It's an interesting list: capital gains cuts are worth about 37 cents to the economy, while an increase in food stamps could net $1.73. A dollar spent on infrastructure will produce around $1.59 in benefit, while making the Bush-era tax cuts permanent would produce only 29 cents. These estimates have shaped the debate about the Obama stimulus plan, and they have lessons for us, too. If we're willing to learn.

One thing you notice as you look at the list is that income supports for poor people have a much more significant (and positive) impact on the economy than aid to rich people and corporations. But what about the investments rich people make in businesses? Step back a moment.

The Zandi estimates are essentially straight expressions of Keynesian economics, and one of Keynes's significant contributions to economics was to point out that savings does not equal investment. A dollar saved is not necessarily a dollar invested.

In classical economics, a dollar in the bank is a dollar invested productively (minus whatever capital requirements the bank has), but does that sound realistic to you?

First of all, bank loans don't always go to productive investment (I know you're shocked) and investment funds don't always come from banks, either. Second, people have different preferences for how they hold their money—cash is different from a CD, for example. And third, changes in the money supply can create big differences between savings and investment, by soaking up excess funds, or supplying more.

Because of this, policies to support rich people are not always helpful. In his landmark, *The General Theory of Employment, Interest and Money*, Keynes wrote, "... the growth of wealth, so far from being dependent on the abstinence [savings] of the rich, as is commonly supposed, is more likely to be impeded by it."

People routinely misunderstand the important points of policy that stem from Keynes's findings. Government spending and progressive taxation aren't good things because they support government workers or "punish" rich people. They are good things because they are how a government can help the economy grow. (Up to a point, of course, a detail Keynes made clear.) Government workers with money to spend will spend it, and that drives the economy. Progressive taxation keeps more money in the hands of the poor and people in the middle, both of whom are more likely to spend their income than rich people are.

Or course, this works in reverse, too. Government layoffs and tax cuts—a perfect summary of the dominant policy prescriptions of both Governor Carcieri's tenure and our recent Assemblies—will make us all poorer in the end.

Keynesian principles aren't just a guide to future action; they are also a way to understand what has happened to us. Between 1997 and 2009, official Rhode Island state government policy has been acting to slowly strangle our own economy, in the name of increasing savings for rich people. In order to cut their taxes, we've raised taxes on poor and middle income families via the property tax, cut education and investment programs, and laid off workers. All of these things have a depressive impact on our economy. We've responded by lowering our aspirations: eliminating advanced courses and special programs at schools, foregoing workforce development projects, letting our infrastructure rot and much more. This, of course, just makes it all worse.

Remarkably, the only solutions on the table seem to be more of the same. My prediction? We'll only get more of the same until we demand that it stop.

Watching out for inflation—and for the CPI

Economic statistics rule our world, but they often don't say what they're widely imagined to say. I'm not with the "lies, damned lies and statistics" crowd, though. Like a lie, it's usually not hard to figure out the truth behind the statistics, but you have to look.

August 2008

HEADLINES DURING THE SUMMER OF 2008 made it clear that we were in for some interesting economic times. But who needs headlines? Most of the important news was pretty clear on any trip to the grocery store. Food prices were up sharply, and since gas prices are mounted in foot-tall numbers on the side of the road, few of us missed the portents there, either. Medical inflation was high, too.

Meanwhile, the Consumer Price Index (CPI) had been quite low for a number of years, and was only up to 4%. It may not have much to do with the level of prices any more, though. The government modifies the index from time to time, but lately they've been making modifications that are convenient—to them.

The value of the CPI is based on a basket of goods, and it's supposed to be comparable from one year to another. The problem is that the goods people buy change. When the CPI was established, cell phones and computers didn't exist, but many of us now consider them essential. That's not all. There are lots of other adjustments that are made. For example, because a cheap computer can do more than a cheap one from ten years ago, the CPI economists say the "effective" price has gone down, even if the actual price has not. (And just try to buy one of those ten-year-old models.)

Housing prices are funny, too. The CPI uses "imputed rent" as its measure of housing costs. For homeowners, this is the rent you might get if you rented out your house. But if you don't rent your house, and pay considerably more than market rent for it, as many people have who are stretching for homeownership, the CPI doesn't match your experience.

In other words, in adjusting the CPI from one year to the next, there are a hundred little decisions to make. In a world where a President's political success is closely tied to the health of the economy, I'm sure it will come as a great shock to you to learn that in virtually every one of those decisions over the past 20 years, the choice was made that would minimize the apparent level of inflation. This leaves the CPI as a good statement of the official line on inflation, but maybe not so much more.

The result is that measures that are tied to inflation—cost of living adjustments in labor contracts and pension systems, as well as budget decisions by incurious legislators and town councilors—fall behind the real level of prices.

Those of us who can recall the 1970's wonder if that kind of inflation is in store. Well, no one really knows, but it's hard to see how it could happen like that now. That is, serious, systemic inflation is caused by rising prices putting pressure on wages which in turn increase prices, and there's a problem with that.

It's pretty clear that rising prices are putting pressure on people, but you can't have a "wage-price spiral" without the wages part. Real wages have stagnated for years, and the truth is that workers in America are in as weak a position as they've been since the 1920's. Between the rise of global trade that has made so many of us competitors with our Asian counterparts, and the loss of union power, where is the upward pressure on wages to come from?[1]

In other words, we're all going to get squeezed by what's coming, and that's particularly bad news for Rhode Island. It is a curious fact of our economy that, while white-collar jobs here pay only a bit less than their counterparts in Massachusetts and Connecticut, blue-collar jobs tend to pay quite a bit less—despite what you hear about unions in Rhode Island.[2] Housing and food costs aren't appreciably lower, so people on the lower end of the scale are going to get squeezed even more here than in our neighboring states.

We're not only talking about poor people here, just people at the low end of the middle and below. Those people obviously don't have a lot of money to spend, but two facts make up for that and give them an outsize effect on our economy. One is that—on average—they save almost nothing and spend virtually everything they get, and the other is that there are a lot of them.

So this is what's likely to happen: people at the lower end of the income scale are going to get squeezed more here in Rhode Island than in our neighboring states simply because they are poorer here. Our state government, so dominated by budget-cutters, will do nothing to help them, and the loss of that spending will help keep our economy in the doldrums longer than our neighbors.

And our Governor and Assembly leaders will wonder, a couple of years hence, why their tax cuts didn't do the trick. But by then they'll find someone to blame.

---

[1]Not to mention that we have become a nation of workers who reflexively side with management in labor disputes, something that will drive future historians nuts as they try to make sense of our wacky society.

[2]See page 105 for more about this, or check it out yourself at *careerjournal.com*.

A stimulating man in a depressing time

Recent economic conditions have caused many to look back to the Great Depression. There is economic instruction available there, but there are some inspiring personal stories, too.

February, 2009

WATCHING THE PROGRESS, of President Obama's stimulus bill as it works its way through Congress is instructive in that you learn a lot about Congress. For example, it's now clear that "centrist" and Republican changes have removed some of the most effective provisions from the package—around half a million jobs—and that they've been allowed to do this because of widespread misunderstanding of what stimulus is.

Here's some review: fiscal stimulus is therapy for a failing economy that we partly owe to British economist John Maynard Keynes, but first to Marriner Eccles, the remarkable chairman of the Federal Reserve Bank from 1934 to 1948. Eccles was a brilliant and thoughtful man who, in 1931, stopped a run on his Utah bank by instructing all his tellers to count the money twice, slowly, and double-check all the signatures. When cash was delivered, borrowed from the Salt Lake Fed, he made the guards bring it through the crowds in the lobby, instead of coming through the back door, defusing the tension by an obvious show of cash. His chain of 28 banks, all over the mountain west, survived the Great Depression without a single failure, while banks all around them fell like autumn leaves.

The experience of the Depression and its near-constant bank panics shook Eccles's understanding of business, and he set out to make sense of events. At the time, the academic world of economics had nothing to offer except assurances that it would all work out somehow. Eccles, who never finished high school, saw this was folly, and saw how his own bank made things worse by restricting loans, shrinking the amount of money circulating in the small towns where his customers lived.

Many economists stop right there, saying experiences like these prove the money supply is the key to the whole thing. But Eccles astutely wrote that the controls on the money supply can only pull, not push. You can constrict the money supply by raising interest rates or calling loans, but doing the reverse—lowering the interest rate—will have no effect if no one wants to borrow. To him, the real question was how to encourage businesses to take the risk of expanding, and the way to do that is to give them customers with the money to buy goods.

That's really how the doctrine of stimulus was born. Keynes came along later and pointed out why it must be so in a more academic and rigorous way, but he was charting territory pioneered by Eccles.

So here's what stimulus is: any spending that produces customers with money to buy goods *and* the inclination to buy some.

That said, there are more and less effective ways to stimulate an economy. For example, money in the hands of poor people usually gets spent immediately, making it do double work (or more) when the recipients spend it again. But money put in the hands of better-off people gets partly saved, making it do half work— or less.[3]

There's more. Money spent investing in things that will change our world has the potential to have a lasting effect without more money later, while money spent on dumb stuff has an effect only while the money is being spent. So investing in public transit and new green technologies is likely to be far more effective than rebuilding roads we've let deteriorate. The first kind will change the game and create new opportunities for private investment, while the second is only covering up for old mistakes, and will create structural problems with paying for maintenance after the stimulus money is gone.

In February, 2009, Governor Carcieri sent a letter to President Obama, criticizing the stimulus. In it, he bragged that he had cut the state payroll by 12%, a brag to say that we've done our part to make the situation worse than necessary. But to our governor, all government spending is bad, so cutting it can only be good. The lessons Eccles found in the Depression are lost on him.

Carcieri's letter went on to say he didn't want the stimulus funds as proposed. What he wants from the federal government is simply road money, tax cuts, and low interest rates.

But the interest rates controlled by the Fed were effectively zero. How do you lower them? And tax cuts? Unless they're targeted at poor and unemployed people, they will be far less effective than investment in things that will change life here for the better. It's not a question of ideology. It's a question of want-

---

[3]See "Our economic woes: Doing it to ourselves" on page 42.

ing the stimulus *to work*—at the lowest cost possible. The Governor's solutions would be more expensive and less effective. Who needs that?

Other Republican suggestions from Congress have been equally inefficient. One idea is a $15,000 tax credit for buying a home. Sadly, buying an existing home isn't putting anyone to work, except for real estate agents. (The sponsor was Georgia Senator Johnny Isakson who used to sell houses.) And what's the point? Is there any house now for sale in Rhode Island where the owner won't accept an offer $15,000 less than the listing? The proposal might put some money into seller's pockets, but they're not likely to spend it all. Again, it's a question of whether you want more bang for your buck, or less.

Marriner Eccles began his life a Mormon Republican believer in rugged individualism and free markets. But he paid attention to the real way the world worked around him, and the Depression showed him the simple lessons his father taught him about the economy were false. Eccles was a big enough man to change his mind when faced with the facts, so change it he did and FDR was impressed enough to invite him into the administration. He helped design important parts of the New Deal, and became chair of the Federal Reserve. Under his leadership, the Fed became the preeminent outpost of the new Keynesian economics in America. Through his career, he let the evidence lead him where it would, and became a champion of doing what works, regardless of ideology. It's an example others could learn from.

How markets fail

You often hear advocates and policy makers talking about how something is obvious, the sort of thing covered in freshman "Economics 101." Such people should stop to consider what economists do in their sophomore years, let alone in graduate school. The answer: they study all the ways in which the Economics 101 picture doesn't work. Here's a survey of some well-known forms of market failure.

February 2009

A N ECONOMIC CRISIS of the magnitude our nation is experiencing (and, as indicators imply, will experience throughout 2009 and beyond) is a serious event. Livelihoods will be lost, opportunities will be passed by and life will get meaner. People will die who might have survived. It's serious business.

Looking for amusement among the wreckage of our nation's economy can thus seem a bit macabre, but it's there for people who appreciate irony. For example, watching free-market-worshipping bankers explain why their bank's assets shouldn't be assessed at market value. Were assessments to be made in the traditional manner, the banks would be instantly insolvent. These same bankers had no trouble using the market value when the market was paying too much.

The deepest irony I know about, though, is that, in the face of a vast and predictable market failure, politicians and policy makers must still pay verbal fealty to the glory of the free market. Barack Obama, in an interview with CNBC in June, 2008, said this:

> "I am a pro-growth, free market guy. I love the market. I think it is the best invention to allocate resources and produce enormous prosperity for America or the world that's ever been designed."

This is the verbal equivalent of wearing a flag pin: the *de rigueur* claim that you aren't some kind of awful subversive. Not being a mind reader, I'm not saying our president doesn't believe it, but he was introducing a critique of the financial markets, calling them "out of balance." In a sensible world, such disclaimers wouldn't be an essential part of a critique, but we don't live in that world, so sometimes wearing a flag pin is easier.

Here's my own version: markets do some things very well. Here's the accompanying truth behind it: not only are there some things markets don't do well, but these are hardly a secret to the economics profession. Sometimes, like now, markets fail. Sometimes, like now, markets fail spectacularly. Sadly, obvious truths like this rarely seem to seep into public discussions of economics.

Let's define market failure. A market is obviously failing when there are sellers who can't find buyers, but there are less obvious forms of failure, too. Buyers who can't find sellers constitute failure in some markets, like housing. This is especially true in situations where the market is for some necessity, again like housing. Economists also speak of different forms of "efficiency." A market is efficient when changes to the distribution of goods and money would use more resources to produce the same quantity of goods, or make some people worse off. Frictionless free markets are always supposed to be efficient, so it's considered a form of market failure when a market is provably inefficient.

The British economist Joan Robinson once wrote:

> "The purpose of studying economics is not to acquire a
> set of ready-made answers to economic questions, but
> to avoid being deceived by economists."[4]

To that end, here is a selection of widely known reasons for markets to fail.

Market failure by information asymmetry

In 2001, George Akerlof, Joseph Stiglitz and Michael Spence won the Nobel Prize for work they did on the effects of "information asymmetry" on markets. This is the situation that arises when sellers know more about the product they're selling than any buyer knows. Because no buyer can be sure if what they're buying is any good, the price of everything is depressed, even the unproblematic good stuff. Akerlof's famous article, "The Market for Lemons," discussed the problem in terms of the used car market, but could there be a better illustration than our current financial crisis?

The financial markets melted down not because of a few million failed mortgages, but because financial derivatives had become so complex that buyers in those markets couldn't be sure

---

[4]*Collected Economic Papers*, MIT Press, 1951–1980, vol. 2, p. 17

they were not inadvertently buying a piece of some worthless asset. The regulators had nothing to say on the matter, and the private ratings agencies have proven themselves completely unworthy of anyone's trust. We have a situation where no one trusts anyone. It's impossible even to look under the hood, so perfectly secure businesses have been unable to find credit. Even state and municipal governments, whose risk of default approaches zero, had to pay elevated interest rates for routine borrowing.

Market failure by market power

It has long been known that markets can also fail because some of the players simply become too powerful. The whole intellectual structure of anti-trust law exists because people came to understand the risks of monopoly a hundred years ago. They understood the risks because Standard Oil, US Steel, the railroad trusts and many others had repeatedly demonstrated them. It was a Republican president who gave us the phrase "malefactors of great wealth."

Today we have Wal-Mart which now owns more than 6% of the retail market. That might not sound like much, but as of 2003, they sold more than 19% of all the groceries in the country, 30% of all the household staples (toothpaste, shampoo, cleaning supplies) and 15% of all the drugs.[5] The result is that in some market categories, if Wal-Mart chooses to exclude some particular producer, that producer is denied a vast amount of the American market. Furthermore Wal-Mart routinely exercises its discretion not to carry items in demand by its customers (most notably in the entertainment and publishing markets).

Market failure by externalities

Not everything has a price, and that's another significant problem with markets. When you drive a car, for example, you are polluting air that you're not paying for. The cost of the pollution is borne by someone else in the form of reduced health or soot they wash off their windowsill or smog. That cost is not worked into the cost of driving, so driving is more expensive than its price. Economists call these factors "externalities" and acknowledge they are present, but also that they can't be accounted for in the standard economics models.

---

[5] *BusinessWeek*, 6 October 2003, "Is Wal-Mart Too Powerful?"

A good that entails externalities is a good whose price does not reflect its cost, so its ultimate distribution cannot be called efficient, by any standard.

Take driving again. Since the price is lower than the cost, the demand for driving is higher than if it were priced appropriately. This results in pollution greater than it should be, not to mention worse traffic.

Another example is the cost of waste disposal. Around 7-8% percent of the waste stream is used or broken consumer goods (not counting disposables or junked cars and trucks), but the manufacturers of those goods don't build the price of disposal into the cost of the goods. So we compare the price of a compact fluorescent light bulb to the cost of an incandescent bulb without considering the cost of disposing of the mercury in the fluorescent bulb.[6]

Market failure by 'irrational' behavior

People don't shop around nearly to the extent supposed by models of economic behavior. For example, electricity deregulation was supposed to herald the coming of market electric rates, with people seeking out the best bargains, driving prices down. Didn't happen. People apparently just aren't that interested in having yet one more thing to shop for. According to National Grid, only 197 of Rhode Island's residential customers have opted for something besides the "standard offer" for their electricity, out of 480,000 customers. In Massachusetts, the numbers were slightly higher: 15,000 out of 1.2 million. In New York, the numbers were much higher, but they have incentives for electricity customers to shop around.

Economists call this kind of thing "irrational" behavior, based on their models of rationality, but that's the easy way out. It often seems there are completely rational reasons for most of what people do, but people's lives are far more complicated than the average economist is willing to credit. The widely remarked failure of market-oriented school choice programs seems to stem from this. In a study of a "large midwestern city's" school choice program conducted by Courtney Bell of the University of Connecti-

---

[6]Or the cost of disease. The Peanut Corporation of America allegedly continued to ship salmonella-contaminated peanut butter because they could be confident that someone else would bear the cost of illness. When it became clear that wasn't true, they fled to bankruptcy court.

cut, she determined that by and large people were choosing ratio-
nally from the choices they perceived. What was notable, though,
is that the choices they perceived were seldom what the program
designers would have thought, taking into account transportation
options, child care dilemmas, gang geography and much more.[7]

Besides, there is a cost in time to shopping around. Is it really
so irrational to value that time enough to want to spend it in some
other way?

Market failure by non-uniform goods

The important economic models of markets are all to do with com-
modity prices: the price of things that are substantially the same
as each other. A bushel of wheat is a bushel of wheat. Of course
there can be slight variations in quality, but a buyer of wheat can
get what he or she wants from almost any seller of wheat. A share
of GM stock is the same, whether it's bought from me or from
someone in China. Economics is pretty good at predicting outcomes in markets like these.

Where economic models routinely fail, though, is in the market for non-uniform goods—and non-uniform buyers. Consider
the job market. What else is a rise in unemployment besides a
mismatch between buyers and sellers? Even in Rhode Island, it's
relatively easy to find employers who want to hire, but can't, either because they can't find people with the skills they need, or
because they can't find anyone to take the wages they can afford
to offer. In other words, job markets fail routinely, and economists
don't say boo about it.

Market failure by market segmentation

An issue related to non-uniform goods is that the market may become segmented. This isn't always a bad thing, but bad things
can come of it. For example, the housing market is highly segmented. The problem lies in the fact that profits for builders are so
much higher at the top end of the market. Builders and investors
all want to serve the top of the market, not the bottom. Top-end

---

[7]Bell, Courtney, *All Choices Created Equal? How Good Parents Select 'Failing'
Schools*, National Center for the Study of Privatization of Education, Teachers College, Columbia University, 2005 working paper. *http://www.ncspe.org/publications_
files/OP106.pdf*

buyers in Providence have hundreds of vacant luxury condos to choose from, but try finding a cheap apartment.

The same thing happened in the car market in the 1980's. Faced with the threat of import restrictions, Japanese auto makers "voluntarily" restricted their US imports, importing only their more expensive and thus more profitable models. The result was that car prices rose from 23 weeks of the average wage in 1979 to 30 weeks by 1986, a rise of 30% in 7 years.[8] Low end buyers learned to make do with used cars.

Why shouldn't markets fail?

This list is hardly exhaustive. Corruption, ill-considered government regulation, and high transaction costs can—and often do—cause markets to fail, too. Many, perhaps most, markets suffer from more than one ill. Housing is segmented and non-uniform, the energy markets suffer from unpriced externalities and market power, and the labor market has information asymmetry in a big way. (It's called resumé fraud.) And all markets are dominated by non-rational buyers and sellers.

What's more, market participants, are constantly trying to find new ways to subvert the classical market forces, because "overcoming market forces" is often another way to say, "getting rich." Given all the traps for them it seems a wonder that markets can function at all. But function they do, many of them.

For a picture of market fiasco, it's hard to do better than the local housing market. Along with the glut of luxury condos, and the shortage of affordable housing, homeless people seeking shelter at Providence's Amos House will inevitably pass more than a handful of boarded-up, foreclosed houses on their way there. These are buyers who can't afford what's on offer passing houses belonging to sellers who can't find buyers. Plain old vanilla economics has perfectly good explanations for market failures like this, but you wouldn't know that from listening to most politicians.

---

[8]Data from Comerica Bank of Detroit. It's back down to 27 these days.

Four

Looking for Investment

Investment, fine. But in what?

Investment brings returns, but it's not as easy as it sounds.

May 2008

IN MAY OF 2008, Governor Carcieri convened a meeting of the newly-reconstituted Economic Policy Council to ask the question, what's going on with our economy and how can we make it better? He was quoted in the *Providence Journal* this way:

> "The state is 'making some real progress,' he said, in making large investments in its infrastructure. He said that the relocation of Route 195, the rebuilding of the Washington Bridge, as well as other major projects amounts to a total investment of $5 billion to $6 billion over four to five years."[1]

This is an impressive figure, but a bit less so when you consider that not a dime of it has gone to create new capacity. We have the I-195 and Sakonnet River bridge projects, both intended to replace bridges that already existed but needed repairs. There's also the highway access to Quonset Point, designed to replace a road with just one stoplight, on which people routinely traveled at 50 miles per hour. This new road shaves about a minute or so off your travel time to Quonset. Then there's the new freight rail to Quonset. There already were rails, but new and taller freight cars and a busier Amtrak schedule were in danger of making them obsolete. We are making the Washington Bridge wider, and that will

---

[1] *Providence Journal*, 22 May 2008, "State leaders focus on troubled economy," T. C. Barmann.

be of comfort to the commuters of Barrington and Rehoboth, but to whom else?

In other words, all that money went to defending the current capacity of our transportation system, not to creating anything new. It didn't go to helping prepare us for a world of more expensive gas, or even for improving travel times by more than a few minutes. When it's all finally done, exactly what will you or any business be able to do that you couldn't do twenty years ago?[2]

The whole point of investment is that when you're done with the investing, you can do more and better stuff than you could before. If that's not true, you may as well be digging holes and filling them in again. Six billion dollars isn't chicken feed, and it paid a lot of construction workers, but what else did we get for it?

When you talk to people about the economic impact of investment, you'll often hear World War II used as an example. It was the government spending of WWII that pulled us out of the Great Depression, you'll hear. I heard that in my first economics class. That's also where I learned that economists love to talk about the importance of big aggregates: the aggregate demand of the US is all the goods we buy in a year, the aggregate production is all the stuff we make. But hidden in those aggregates are some pretty important details, and we overlook them at our risk.

Government spending on WWII and the Cold War pulled us out and kept us out of the Great Depression, but look at what that spending did. Spending on aircraft created a new domestic aviation industry. Spending on nuclear energy created a new nuclear power industry (for better or worse). Spending on high-speed electronics and communication technology created a new electronics industry and ultimately created the computer. All this spending, and much more, was investment that transformed our lives, and the nation. It's no wonder that the 1950's were a boom time in the American economy.

According to the textbook macroeconomic analysis, however, all that really mattered was the aggregate level of government spending. The theory is that high enough spending will spur

---

[2]People routinely point out to me that moving the bridge will free up a lot of land for development in Providence's jewelry district. This is nice, and some people will earn a lot of money from it, but it's not as if there was a shortage of usable land in Providence. The project also demolished some occupied buildings, at least one of which was filled with small business startups. The economy won't profit by this new land, though certainly a few lucky investors will.

investment, even if the spending isn't investment itself. But to imagine that market-driven investment would have been as transforming is missing the trees for the forest; the details are important. Instead of the transformational investments we made, we might have created minor improvements to existing products, or invented self-freezing popsicles instead.

Government investment in aviation and radar during and after the war made passenger air travel possible, government research in information transmission led to the development of all kinds of telecommunications technologies (long-distance telephones, radio and other wired communication links), and government investigations in cryptography and electronics made computers possible. To imagine that the only important variable here is the sheer *amount* of this investment strains credulity. Again, this episode is generally used to demonstrate the efficacy of deficit spending, with little regard for what the money was spent on. To a typical US-trained economist, government spending is government spending is government spending. The bottom line is all that matters, and don't bother us with details.

This is why someone like Rhode Island's Governor can boast about spending $6 billion on roads as if it will make an ounce of difference to our economy over the long term. Sure that's a lot of construction crew salaries, but what else did it get us?

Once a week or so, I find myself navigating the high-tech canyons of Kendall Square, in Cambridge, hard by MIT. As I walk down Main Street, I'm surrounded by research institutes and technology companies of every stripe. Huge new buildings have sprung up (and are springing up) since I last spent much time there, 15 years ago. The growth and activity are nearly breathtaking. MIT is a phenomenal place in many ways, but one thing it isn't is an accident. MIT happened because people who cared about science and technology invested time and money to make it happen.

Here's what they didn't do to create MIT: skimp on the library's book budget; encourage the early retirement of dozens of faculty who will be "replaced" with adjunct faculty without research funding or sometimes even a campus presence; fail to support research faculty between grants; close departments that weren't "making" enough money for the university; and build shiny new buildings without a commitment to staff them. We have done all that at the University of Rhode Island. Our university could be an economic engine—check out the industrial area near the oceanography school sometime—but we need to support it.

So when you hear the Governor boasting about our investment in roads and bridges, think to yourself what our state might be like had we just patched those bridges instead and used the leftover money to invest in a real transformation of our higher education.

At the same EPC meeting, Robert Carothers, the president of URI put it best:

> "Last year, we were 50th in the nation in investment and research. We were the only state in the nation that didn't increase higher education funding from year to year...No amount of smooth talking makes those things go away."[3]

Taxes and investment

Some recent economic issues eerily recall problems identified during the Great Depression.

SUPPOSE ONE DAY you found in the mail notice of a bequest from a long-lost aunt. The sad news, of course, is that your aunt had passed away, but the happy news is that you can have $60,000 from her estate, on the condition that you invest it in something productive. After the jubilation fades, you contact the estate attorney and learn that "productive" means no stocks or real estate.[4] With those rules, would you know what to do with this money?

If you have trouble thinking of something you could invest in, you're not alone. After financial investments and real estate, what else is there? Real business, that's what, but therein lies a big problem.

A generation ago, Rhode Island boasted dozens of small plastic companies, each of which owned a handful of injection- or blow-molding presses. Many of these businesses were started to

---

[3] *Providence Journal, ibid.* 22 May 2008.

[4] And no drugs or high-stakes poker, either. Turns out she was kind of a prude.

fulfill demand from Hasbro or the costume jewelry industry, but came to serve a national market for plastic parts. The barriers to entry were relatively low—some space and money for a couple of machines—and the demand was high. Those shops required the services of skilled machinists to make molds and repair machines, creating opportunities for others to invest in machine tools. They also required material suppliers and warehousing facilities, creating more opportunities for investment there, too.

All of these were opportunities for productive investment on a scale that could be embraced by someone with a small bequest, a small collection of partners, or an uncle called upon by his nephew (or niece). Banks could sometimes be involved, but many businesses start with capital raised less formally, through family and friends.[5] Other industries provide similar opportunities: fishing boats, for example, as well as retail stores and restaurants.

In 2009, which of these opportunities remain? Hasbro has exported all its plastic molding jobs to China, lots of the presses and stamps of the costume jewelry industry have disappeared, and the fishing industry has taken a nose-dive. The retail and restaurant options remain, but in a world dominated by Wal-Mart, Home Depot and McDonald's, which are the retail niches that can be profitable on a small scale? The existence of both Staples and OfficeMax means that neither is a monopoly, but that's meager consolation to someone who wants to start a stationery store.

Of course there are new niches to replace some of these old ones, but if you find one, you'll likely find yourself competing in a global market from the beginning. Now that it's routine to find retail via the internet and to contract suppliers on the other side of the world, competition is a bit more forbidding than it was in a more parochial world. This is not necessarily comforting to a prospective investor, and so can ruin an otherwise promising opportunity.

You can see this story reflected in investment statistics pub-

---

[5]A 1998 study of the Atlantic provinces of Canada used a random sample of businesses to conduct a survey about the use of informal investments. The report's author found a surprisingly high percentage of new businesses had used some kind of informal money as startup capital. Using that report's estimates of activity, Rhode Island might see around $60-65 million in informal investments in new businesses each year. See "Informal Venture Capital Investment in Atlantic Canada" by A. Ellen Farrell for the Atlantic Canada Opportunities Agency, February 1998.

lished by the Federal Reserve as part of their "Flow of Funds" reports. When you look at aggregate investment statistics, you see the peaks and valleys of our recent economic history, worrisome, certainly, though not necessarily panic-inducing. The current levels of nonresidential fixed investment (like factories and machines, but also real estate) are between 10% and 11% of our Gross Domestic Product (GDP). Despite having dropped dramatically since September 2008, they are still higher than they were during the postwar boom, so nothing to worry about, right? We may be going through a dip, but with investment so strong, it's just a matter of time. Is that it?

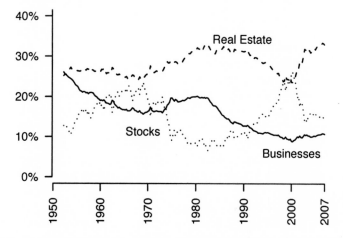

Figure 4.1: Investments as a proportion of overall household assets. The solid line is the value of household ownership of non-corporate businesses: partnerships, LLCs and small businesses. The other two lines show the proportion of household assets in real estate and the stock market. (Source: Federal Reserve Z.1 Flow of Funds reports)

Well, maybe. For one thing, fixed investment includes real estate, and the value of the huge (and now crashing) commercial real estate market may have been propping up the investment number. Over the past three decades, the escalating value of commercial real estate was crucial to keeping that highly-leveraged industry afloat. The recent bankruptcy filings of General Growth, the biggest mall owner in the country, have shown how much the industry depended on credit just to stay afloat in the good times. The "investment" was huge, but the reason economists think investment is important is because it is the basis of future production. Even if its construction is a big and expensive proposition, does a mall really belong in the same category as a factory?

That's not the only troubling issue. Another hides in the share of household assets taken up by the partnerships and sole proprietorships that make up the bulk of small businesses. As a share of all household assets, business equity has been declining ever since 1950, except for a bump in the early 1970's. It rose slightly during the Bush II years, but a closer look shows this was primarily a result of appreciating real estate values, and had little to do with the number or health of those businesses. You can see the story in the decline of business investment in Figure 4.1. The difference has been made up mostly with pension assets and real estate. To a lesser extent stocks and other financial investments like bank deposits have helped.

You can also see the decline in business value in the mirror nature of the real estate and stock lines. When real estate goes down, the stock market goes up and vice versa, an effect that has been enhanced in recent years. Why? Because there are so few other places to put the money. According to the Fed's numbers, a lot of the volatility of the real estate market of the last couple of decades can be blamed on this decline. Money that used to be locked up in relatively non-liquid business assets is now in investments where it can be moved much more easily, and we see that in the real estate market swings.

In other words, much of the investment supposed to be holding up our economy may not be what it used to be, nor even what it seems.

Debating the lack of investment opportunity

In the 1930's and 1940's a perceived decline in opportunities for productive investment was a hot topic among economists. This was one of the big puzzles presented by the Great Depression, where it appeared that there was plenty of money to invest, but nothing worth investing in. Alvin Hansen, a Harvard economist who became the most prominent interpreter of Keynes's theories in America, theorized that it had to do with the end of our nation's geographical expansion, the slackening of population growth and a supposed tendency for new technologies to have lower capital costs than old ones. The combination meant that what opportunities for investment were available were already filled, and that over time, less and less capital could be productively invested due to the declining cost.[6]

The theory was satisfying to few, since America's dramatic expansion in area stopped decades before the Depression, population growth seems to have little to do with economic growth (as we see in places like Bangladesh or Haiti) and the idea that investment had come to cost less in real terms was really only speculative and couldn't be demonstrated.

One of Hansen's chief antagonists was Joseph Schumpeter, the famous Austrian economist (who was by then also teaching at Harvard). His perspective, stated baldly, was that the risk-averse culture of the welfare state had sapped the vital juices of the entrepreneurs needed to make the capitalist system work. To him, the problem wasn't so much that the opportunities weren't there, but that there was a shortage of bold entrepreneurs ready to use them. Or maybe it was just the labyrinth of new government regulations that kept them from bestowing the full measure of their talents on society. But in truth, Schumpeter was never able to make this into an argument supported by data, so he only won over people already inclined to support his perspective on social legislation.[7]

The debate raged, but meanwhile, World War II started and ended, and after it there was a tremendous burst of investment as companies rushed to fulfill four years of pent-up demand. Suddenly, the debate between Hansen and Schumpeter seemed quaint. This was Keynes's answer to the stagnation problem: if there's enough demand, investment will simply happen. His explanation of the Depression, and the one most widely accepted today, is that there simply wasn't enough money in the hands of people who wanted to buy stuff. Deficit spending—the way we financed the war—was a way to put it there, and the increase in demand created the opportunities to invest.[8] Today, the problem of vanish-

---

[6]For more, see Alvin Hansen, "Full Recovery or Stagnation?" W. W. Norton, 1938, Chapter 19.

[7]For a good review, see "Monopolization and the Decline of Investment Opportunity", by George W. Hildebrand, American Economic Review, Vol. 33, No. 3 (Sep. 1943) pp. 591-601. Without data, Schumpeter's theory about the effects of the welfare state became part of his theorizing about grand cycles of social change, a part of his intellectual legacy that is perhaps justifiably neglected.

[8]But see "Investment, fine. But in what?" on page 56.

ing investment opportunities is pretty much a dead issue among
economists.

But should it be?

National Income Accounts

If Keynes was right about the Depression, many economists con-
jectured he was right about other things, too. But his theory depended on things that were hard to measure: the size of the economy, the amount of spending in a whole nation, the total number
of people working, and so on. Enterprising American economists
began to build a bureaucracy to measure and estimate these numbers, in order to learn how to avoid depressions, instead of just
enduring them. Their success means that today we can draw pic-
tures like the one in Figure 4.1 on page 61.

Economists call these numbers the "national income accounts"
and their creation was one of the important achievements of this
new generation of economists. You hear about these numbers all
the time, in the news, in official reports and more. They are a
(large) collection of aggregate measures of spending, investment,
production and lending, all of which together are used to calculate
the size of our economy, or the Gross Domestic Product (GDP).
You see GDP used not just as a measure of size, but also as a proxy
for its health. When GDP is growing, all is supposedly well, and
when it shrinks, that's a recession, at least officially.

It's important to remember, though, that these measurements
and calculations were developed in service of a particular theory,
the Keynesian theory, of how the economy works.[9] We have since
modified our understanding of the economy several times, but
the national income accounts remain fundamentally the same as
when they were first designed.

There are problems with these numbers. For example, no one
has figured out how to get such things as the costs of pollution

---

[9]Or rather the "bastard Keynesian" theory, as Cambridge economist, and
Keynes's colleague, Joan Robinson put it. By this she meant Keynes's 'stimulate
demand with government deficits' view, which was readily incorporated into a
mathematical framework not terribly distant from the neo-classical economics that
preceded it. But the economics profession that was able to incorporate this much
found itself unable to accommodate his more controversial insights into the effects
of power relations, uncertainty and "animal spirits" on the economy. It's worth
remembering that "Keynesian economics," as it is commonly understood, leaves
out about half of what Keynes himself thought. A good account of this is George
Akerlof and Robert Shiller's book, *Animal Spirits* (Princeton Univ. Press, 2009).

and *into* the calculations, or the benefits of devastation *out*. Pollution involves loss of productivity (as when people get sick or can't work) and loss of land and opportunity, but there is no transaction where these costs are paid, so they don't show up in the calculations. Hurricane Katrina was a net *gain* to the economy in terms of GDP, since there were truckloads of lumber and mobile homes to buy, and all the other supplies for rebuilding New Orleans. In gross economic terms, we could boost the economy of the rust belt by burning Cleveland to the ground, but it's not clear how that would make us collectively better off.

What about when GDP shifts from one category to another? According to the mainstream of economic thought, what's important is the total demand in the economy, not the composition of the total. Shifts like this are therefore not deemed important. There are serious problems with this perspective, even if the overall theory has been a fruitful source of useful insights into the functioning of the economy.

There are two important questions about any spending: where it came from and where it's going. Destination first: the GDP includes spending on durable goods, but consider the contrast between an upholstered chair and an electric car, both durable goods. Given modern assembly techniques, they both require a comparable amount of labor for their final assembly (with less automation, the chair takes longer, really). But one of them also requires extensive design and engineering services, and manufactured components from many different sources: circuit boards, components, batteries, windshields, bumpers. Producing an electric car requires a much more varied collection of suppliers. The purchase of an electric car ripples through the economy much farther than the purchase of the chair.

These are retrospective effects, though. By the time you buy the car, most of those suppliers will have been paid (though not all), and those purchases will have been incorporated into the aggregate statistics. But what of the demand that your purchase *will* create?

A million upholstered chairs will provide a million places to sit. A million electric cars will demand the creation of charging facilities, specialized repair shops, companies to offer improvements to the technology and other companies to print "Get A Charge Out of Life" bumper stickers. A successful investment in satisfying demand for comfy chairs will find itself at the root of lots of new chairs, while a successful investment in satisfyings demand for electric cars will find itself at the root of whole new industries. The potential impact is far greater for the car, and this effect is not captured by our aggregate statistics.

What about the source of investment? Does that make a difference? It does, and you can ask anyone who's been involved in a software startup. This was explained to me by an executive at a company I consulted with once. One day he told me, somewhat to my surprise, how pleased he was have been able to reject what I thought sounded like a generous financing offer from a venture capital firm. He explained to me the world of difference between venture capitalists. Some make the construction of the business their priority and others give the precedence to cashing out. One group populates boards with people who have the expertise to grow a company, looking to make management stronger and smarter. Another group simply finds board members willing to pull the trigger when the VC boss says it's time to sell. Both groups have made millions, but the first group is far more likely to make a lasting impact on the world.

To avoid exactly these complications, it's commonplace advice in those circles to finance a company's startup with debt—to yourself, to friends or to relatives—if you possibly can. It seems almost too banal an observation to be worth stating, but a company's priorities are shaped by its funding, whether that funding is from business revenue or venture capital.

In other words, it not only matters where an investment goes, it matters where it comes from. Local investment in a small-scale business is going to provide that business with a very different set of priorities than would investment through distant intermediaries.[10] This is why the decline in household investment in businesses is a worrisome development, and it's also why the economic wisdom about aggregate quantities can lead to hare-brained policies.

The source of capital has local implications, too. When a local business opens, there is all kinds of investment that translates

---

[10]It's possible to read the foreclosure crisis as a laboratory demonstration of how much it matters where the capital comes from. The big banks and institutional investors who packaged and repackaged their loan portfolios, selling them to distant parties, were responsible for almost all the foreclosures and failures. Small banks who didn't participate in that market, and who relied on local judgments about local residents, have survived the crisis just fine.

into the local purchase of goods: tools, computers and machinery, perhaps, but also desks, chairs and heating equipment. Some of these goods are purchased nearby, and so the investment turns into spending. When a national chain opens a new store, there will be some investment, but not much local. Most of it happens back at corporate headquarters, where corporate architects draw up the plans, corporate purchasers plan the furnishing and corporate construction staff come out to supervise local crews. Investment today stimulates demand tomorrow, but if investment in Rhode Island today stimulates demand tomorrow in Georgia or Arkansas, then what good is that to us?[11]

The aggregate measures of investment utterly fail to capture the a whole host of differences among investment sources, not least the difference between local, direct investment and distant, mediated investment. But the dominant economic theories are based upon these aggregate measures. For people who believe in that theory, it is a conundrum that, until the recent downturn, we had relatively healthy levels of investment, but high unemployment nonetheless. For people who see a qualitative difference between investment in a new Home Depot and investment in a local hardware store, the conundrum is about the economists.

Consider the future

This is not just an idle excursion into economic theory. State and local taxes have been cut time after time to "stimulate the economy." We cut capital gains taxes to encourage investment, we've cut the income tax on the richest of the rich to encourage them to live and invest here. But these prescriptions presuppose a shortage of capital and a shortage of investors. On the contrary, the data—from the Federal Reserve, from the Providence Assessor's Office and Rhode Island Housing,[12] and from our own eyes— clearly show that our poor state is awash in capital sloshing back and forth between the stock market and real estate. Our economy

---

[11]Even when there are attractive opportunities, another problem comes from the concentration of capital. Managing money takes time and effort, and finding good investments is not easy. An investor with a million to invest will likely not have the time to look at enough $10,000 and $20,000 investments to fill a portfolio. You can employ brokers to look for you, but the commissions they'll earn mean that the investments they do find would have to be more profitable than most small retail can be in order make it worthwhile.

[12]See "Speculation speculation" on page 92.

is a capital-producing machine, creating a tremendous reserve of investable funds each year, but providing few productive ways to invest it.

A huge propensity to save[13] plus nowhere to invest is a recipe for stagnation. This is money waiting to be spent, but sitting idle instead, uninvested and unspent. And tax cuts won't help. Our problem isn't a lack of rich people or a lack of money to invest. Our problem is that, like it or not, the business opportunities that once were easy to find are no longer so easy. If the state wants to help stimulate new investment, helping create still more capital is absolutely the wrong way to do it.

How, then, do we stimulate new investments? Promoting demand is one way. This means getting money into the hands of whoever will spend it usefully. This might mean consumers, it might mean businesses and it might even mean government.[14] It's worth spending time to think about the kinds of demand worth stimulating, though, because it matters.

Beyond what we already know about the market and our society is the stuff that hasn't been invented yet, or perhaps not even conceived. In the 21st century, good ideas are more valuable than capital. Protecting and promoting people who have those ideas and finding ways to connect them to investors would be more valuable than simply rewarding investors who haven't done anything yet. But even these are dicey strategies.

It's a big leap, but consider this: in economic terms, the quality of public and higher education is the only real difference between Massachusetts and Rhode Island. We have the same climate, nearly the same location, the same raw materials and so on. But Massachusetts, over the past forty years, has become a much wealthier state. If not by education, than what else?

In other words, one proven strategy for coming up with new investments—possibly the only one we know will work—is to educate our children to find them. So teach them about the rest of the world so that they will be able to see opportunities that others don't. Teach them about technology and science so they'll be able to exploit the opportunities that others can't. Teach them art and music and theatre so they'll be able to think of opportunities that

---

[13]Economics jargon for the ability of an economy to generate investable funds.

[14]For example, public transit is an market niche currently not served very well by US manufacturers, and the buyers are most likely to be governments.

others cannot. Instead of continuing to shower rich people with tax breaks they probably won't (or can't) use to our advantage, why don't we try that?

Cut it and will they come?

Debates about tax policy are often conducted as if no one has ever rigorously studied the question of what makes businesses settle in one location or another. But this is hardly the case, and Rethinking Growth Strategies: How State and Local Taxes and Services Affect Economic Development *by Robert G. Lynch of the Economic Policy Institute (2004) is one of the best reviews I've run across of the academic literature about business location decisions.*

April 2005

FIDELITY, ALPHA-BETA, GTECH, American Power Conversion, the Providence Place Mall. All of these corporations have received special tax concessions from the state of Rhode Island over the past few years. Some of these deals work out as planned, and others don't. But they all cost money. Sometime concessions are extracted in response, but the follow-up to those concessions is usually weak or nonexistent. (Where is the independent downtown movie theatre once promised by the mall? How many APC jobs eventually went to welfare recipients? Where's the massive expansion Fidelity predicted?)

Rhode Island sits squarely among other states in the use of these concessions. We're part of a national trend, and it's part of the reason why the business taxes growth since 1990 has been negative once you correct for inflation. But the underlying logic behind these concessions has always been more than a bit suspect. Businesses create jobs, yes, but businesses also rely on police and fire protection, require good roads and other transportation, expect not to have to teach their employees to read. These services are important to the businesses and to the people who work in them.

Proponents of tax concessions as a growth strategy point to cases like the Mercedes-Benz factory in Alabama, which now supports a few thousand jobs. Opponents mention that the state paid well over $150,000 for each of those jobs. Then they point to South Dakota, which is sort of like Minnesota without the high taxes, but also without the all the companies and all the jobs Minnesota has. Over the past few years, as the debate over these kinds of concessions has intensified, the number of studies reporting on the problem has multiplied. Now comes Robert Lynch, of the Economic Policy Institute, with a survey of several dozen such studies, in *Rethinking Growth Strategies: How State and Local Taxes and Services Affect Economic Development*

And, well, the plot's a bit thin. He really has only one theme, but boy does he hammer on it. His point: that the services government provides are at least as important to economic growth as the taxes on business, and usually much more so. What he finds, in wading through the econometric studies, the interview studies and the survey studies, is that there isn't really *any* persuasive data to make the case that tax concessions have a net positive benefit to growth.[15] The only studies he finds that show evidence of a positive effect are a couple of econometric studies—Bartik is one prominent name—that implicitly assume that you can lower taxes *without* reducing spending on public services.

Timothy Bartik, an economist with the Upjohn Institute in Kalamazoo, Michigan, has published several technical papers on the subject of firm location decisions. In typical economist fashion, he applies sophisticated mathematical techniques to extract trends from the raw survey data. But also in typical economist fashion, he either doesn't realize, or hopes we won't notice, that his method is meant for teasing apart the importance of *independent* variables. Taxes and public services, for example, are not independent. Lowering one tends to lower the other. By treating the two as independent, Bartik's work is really asking whether it's good to lower taxes while keeping services constant. You don't need a degree in economics to see that (a) this is appealing to everyone, and (b) this is usually impossible. In other words, Bartik's work is a nearly perfect example of highly sophisticated bad math.

In a similarly efficient fashion, Lynch disposes of the business-climate argument for tax concessions. What evidence, he asks, is there that a "signal" sent by a tax cut will be received by the population of businesses it's aimed at? Reviewing the literature, he

---

[15]Another good review of this literature is in the dissents that make up part of the final report of the 2009 Governor's Blue Ribbon Commission on Tax Reform.

concludes pretty much none, and if the tax concession is a small one, any conceptual effect will be swamped by the practical effect of much more significant costs. The sad truth: in the scale of expenses most businesses have, state taxes are pretty much peanuts when compared to rents, supplies, marketing, transportation, and even federal taxes.

Besides, "sending a signal" is a perverse way to sell a policy, especially when you're bankrupting the state in the process. Who gets the signal, and what do they think it is? The signal received might not be the one sent. We might mean to say, "We're pro-business here." But the signal received might be, "We're suckers here. Take us for a ride." Miscommunication like this happens all the time—think about dating—and it often starts with an ill-considered gift.

Lynch moves on to systematically tackle pretty much all the arguments used to justify these concessions. Like toy ducks in a shooting gallery, he lines them up and bang, down they go. The business-climate argument, bang! The competitiveness argument, bang! The supply-side argument, the tax-burden argument and the demand-side argument, bang, bang, bang! Some of these canards are so tired and so often seen hanging around the state house that a citizen among those who pay for these concessions can hardly keep from cheering as they go down.

There are a couple of caveats throughout, where you can see that Rhode Island may be one of the places where the argument against incentives isn't as strong as in, say, Minnesota. We are quite small, as if anyone could forget it, and Massachusetts and Connecticut are quite convenient. But slightly more equivocal is hardly the same as overturning the argument, and his overall point is just as valid here as anywhere: the business of government is providing public services—safety, education, health—and the better and more efficient they are, the better for everyone, businesses and people, both. And when the services are threatened, it's not at all good for either.

Five

Fleeing the Cities

What happened to our towns?

Towns grow. Who knew? More important, who knew this has important budgetary consequences? Well, anyone who spent five minutes thinking about it, that's who. But a lot of people make a lot of money from suburban sprawl, so a lot of people don't think about it. As Upton Sinclair put it, "It is difficult to get a man to understand something, when his salary depends on his not understanding it!"

February 2009

WHEN I WAS 16, I went SCUBA diving off Jamestown a few times with my friends Nat and Phil. Once, right after we came off the bridge, we headed south to Fort Wetherill, with Phil driving. We passed a police car headed north and a moment or two later Nat said, "There," and pointed at another police car, parked on a side road. "Great," said Phil, and floored it. As we hurtled down the narrow country lane at about 70, I gripped the seat and asked what he meant. "Jamestown only has two police cars," he laughed, "so we can do what we want now."

Needless to say, Jamestown has more than two police cars, now. But why? Did they expand their police force only in order to pad the town payroll? That's what Governor Carcieri would like you to think. Last week, in his State of the State address, the Governor clucked his tongue at the cities and towns, because over the past 20 years, while the state payroll has dropped by a quarter, the total number of municipal employees has gone up by 38%. Shocking, isn't it?

Well, not really. What's shocking is that someone thinks he can run the state with "information" like this: half-digested red meat to be thrown to the angry mobs of talk-radio callers. Let's get real. Town payrolls have gone up because towns have grown, and because of requirements imposed on them. Jamestown has twice as many year-round residents, and many more summer houses, than it did back in the days of two police cars. Rhode Island has about the same number of people as a generation ago, but our little towns are bigger and our cities are smaller. We have spread out across the landscape, and that has real consequences.

Want to know what else Jamestown has that it didn't have a generation ago? Special-ed students who used to be wards of the state, attending the Ladd School. Having special-needs children educated with other children is a *good* thing, but it's not free. When the state closed Ladd, do you remember how the state gave that money to cities and towns for special education? Yeah, neither do I.

What else didn't Jamestown have back then? Clean-water mandates imposed by the EPA, comprehensive planning laws, bus monitors on school buses, homeland security mandates on public safety departments and more. Here's the thing, though: all of these requirements were imposed for a reason. Clean water, good planning, and public safety are all important. Whether the benefits are worth the money is always a debate worth having, but it's crazy to pretend these mandates came from nowhere.

Despite his absurd scolding tone, Governor Carcieri has done us all a service by putting his finger on a big source of the state's fiscal problems. A state that relies so much on local revenue—property taxes—is poorly positioned to deal with the effects of people moving around.

When people leave a town, it takes a while to cut the expenses of the services they used, if it's possible at all. If you have a hundred kids in a fifth grade, that's four classrooms. If ten of those children move away, that's still four classrooms, but with less money to pay for them. If a fire station is established to deal with a neighborhood of 500 houses, a town can't close it just because 50 of those houses are now vacant. And a shrinking town doesn't need a smaller police department. (If anything, experience shows it needs a larger one.)

There's nothing at all mysterious about this phenomenon. Economists and business types refer to it as the "marginal cost," the cost of the last student taught or the last house protected. In any business, the relevant cost for some good usually isn't the average cost of that good, but the marginal cost. The marginal cost of adding a single person to an almost-full airplane is very low, even though the average cost of the passengers on the plane is large, and that's why airlines like to fly full planes.[1]

The opposite side of the coin is just as telling. A family with two school-age children moving to some rural town will likely cost that town as much as $30,000 in services, but provide only a fraction of that in taxes. New construction often requires new traffic lights, new water lines, new sewer lines and more. These expenses are never covered by the new tax revenue and seldom even covered by occasionally imposed "developer impact fees."

In other words, the movement of people from one town to another can raise taxes in *both* towns. In one town they go up because there are a shrinking number of people to support the same services, while in the other they go up because new residents require more services than they pay for. In a world where cities and towns got more support from the state, this wouldn't matter so much.

While looking into the possible benefits of school district consolidation, I spent some time last year with the budget for Fairfax County, Virginia, part of the DC suburbs, and said to have a fabulous school system.[2] Their school department has about as many students in it as the 36 school departments in Rhode Island. Their spending on administration isn't so much lower than ours, though, so the potential benefit of combining school districts isn't nearly what proponents claim. What they do have, however, is a size that insulates them against the movement of people. When people move from the near suburbs of DC to the farther suburbs, they're moving from one side of Fairfax to the other. The county and school department are still collecting their taxes. Their kids might have a longer bus ride, but that's the only adjustment

---

[1] This is a fairly basic point of economics or business, so it's curious to note that it is so often ignored, even by people who want me to be impressed by their business acumen. For example, the formula that funds charter schools in Rhode Island instructs school districts to pay the *average* cost of their students for each student who attends a charter school. Of course the school district doesn't save that much money, so the net effect is that the charter school is paid for by the students who don't attend it.

[2] The choice of Fairfax County was pretty random, motivated largely by some friends of mine who had moved to Rhode Island from there, and were endlessly comparing the two. That said, the Fairfax school department does appear to be very good. Three of their high schools appear on US News and World Report's list of the nation's 100 top high schools. Other rankings seem similarly impressive.

that needs to be made. Here, though, when a family moves from Cranston to Exeter, they're helping send Cranston's finances into a tailspin, and creating pressures on Exeter's budget that Exeter might not have wanted.

Proponents of school and town consolidation are like the blind squirrel that accidentally finds a nut from time to time. They are on to something valuable, but for the wrong reasons. We don't need super towns like Wesconnaug (an ill-fated proposal to combine several towns along the Connecticut border) or to combine town administrations. We need to come up with a way to fund municipal services that can withstand having people move from one town to another. Not only would this keep a better lid on the growth of taxes, but could ease the pressure on towns to make dumb land-use decisions simply because they need the tax money.

When people move, the cost can be high

When people move, the local cost is high. The tension between the state and the municipalities is high these days. But no one seems to ask why cities and towns have a hard time making their budget targets.

May 2007

WHEN DISCUSSING THE STATE BUDGET, it's almost impossible to avoid discussions of municipal finance. Between education aid, building aid, support of teacher pensions, payments in lieu of taxes, and all the other forms of local aid, quite a lot of the funds raised by state taxes are expended at the cities and towns, or on their behalf. Figuring out the exact number is a challenge, since a number of money sources seem to straddle definitions. Is establishing a statewide math curriculum aid to towns? What about federal grants that pass through the state en route from Washington to Foster? And what about teacher retirement assistance funds: given to the towns in order to be paid right back to the state? The Governor and legislators are inclined to be generous in their counting, and by their count the state budget counts $285 million in direct aid and tax money that comes from the state and goes to cities, towns and fire districts. As of 2009, there is another $910 million in aid to schools (including those pension fund payments). All told, as of 2007, about a third of the taxes the state collects go to support the state's local governments, and these make up between 15% and 45% of city and town revenues, depending on the town.

This, of course, is a tremendous bone of contention at the statehouse, where it is widely assumed that local governments accept the state's money to use it as toilet paper back at town hall. This may seem a harsh assessment, but consider the evidence from the FY08 budget proposal:

- The Governor proposed to award all the state-run public schools budget increases of 6-10%, since that's how much their costs rose. The municipal schools got 3%, even though their costs likely went up 6-10%, too.

- The Senate last year enacted strict limits on town budgets without promising any compensating money, as if to say, "We're not sure what you're spending money on, but it certainly isn't very important."

- The Governor's 2008 budget Executive Summary has a heading "Encouraging Local Government Efficiency" which is really a proposal to hire three new state workers to help give towns less money to build schools.

- The 2008 budget contains no increase in non-education local aid, except for pass-through money over which the state has no control. Yet the state budget will go up, as will the municipal budgets.

Consider this, too: Over the past 17 years, the property taxes collected by all the towns in the state have risen, on average, at about 4.5% per year. The state income tax collections are up by an average of 5.4% per year. But the income tax *rates* are down as much as 40%, depending on your income (see Figure 5.1) while property tax bills have skyrocketed everywhere. For all the groaning about tight budgets heard around the statehouse, the state has a far easier time earning the revenue it needs to operate than do the towns.

The usual villains identified in the conventional tale are public employee unions, along with too-pliant city officials. Certainly the unions are part of the story, but are they really so strong? Are they

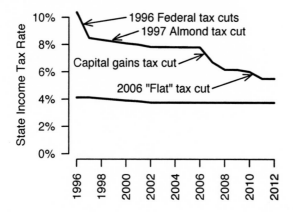

Figure 5.1: Rhode Island income tax rates. The bottom line is the tax rate applied to a family with taxable income at the median. (Half the families in the state have higher incomes, and half have lower incomes.) You can see the effect of the Almond tax cuts in the rate decline between 1998 and 2002. The upper line shows the tax rate applied to a family in the top 1% of income, who had about a third of their income from capital gains. (Source: RI General Laws)

really so evil? Here's one problem with the story. If you believe that unions are the problem, or that bad management is, then why are some towns doing so much better than others? Union contracts statewide differ in the details, but not in the broad strokes, and city and town managements seem to be drawn from the same corps of people. North Kingstown recently replaced its town manager, who moved on to manage things in Coventry. To replace him, they hired a guy who used to be the town manager of Middletown. Middletown, in turn, is now run by one of his former deputies, another of whom oversees finances in Portsmouth. Certainly there are differences among these guys, but to imagine that they are the biggest differences between towns seems unlikely.

A Tale of Two Towns

It's interesting to compare Portsmouth and Middletown. These two towns have about the same population, sit next to each other on a small island, and have about the same tax rate.[3] That's about

---

[3]Ed. note: the rates have diverged slightly since 2007, with Middletown's rate slightly higher than Portsmouth's as of 2009. The rest of the differences and similarities—politics, bond rating, island—remain as they were.

where the similarities end. Portsmouth is in the throes of a fiscal crisis, and is skirting disaster as it tries to squeeze through the current fiscal year, while Middletown has just had its bond rating upgraded to one of the highest in the state. Portsmouth has a well-organized political faction, the "Portsmouth Concerned Citizens" who last year engineered a substantial cut to the school budget at a town financial meeting. Middletown has concerned citizens, but nothing nearly as well organized or militant.

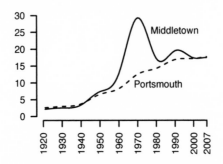

Figure 5.2: The population of Middletown and Portsmouth (in thousands). The two towns are the same size now, but they got there in very different ways, and the fact has long-term repercussions for their budgets.

When you ask people in each town what's so different about them, they'll point to the fact that Middletown has more commercial property and this lowers the tax rate on residential property. Unfortunately for this theory, the residential tax rates in the two towns are within a few percent of each other. (Due to the budget disputes, Portsmouth has had three rates this year.)

Here's one difference between them: they are the same size now, but they got there in very different ways. In the heyday of the Navy's presence in Newport, Middletown's population was almost twice what it is now. Portsmouth, on the other hand, has been growing at a pretty good clip since the 1940s, though it has leveled off in recent years.

Digging a little further into their history, it turns out that Middletown suffered a fiscal crisis a few years ago, at the end of the 1990's. As was noted before, their finances are fine now, but for a while they were looking at the same kinds of problems as beset Portsmouth today.

When analyzing real-world towns, there are a million variables to consider, and it's difficult to figure out which are the important ones. When scientists are faced with problems like these, they often turn to computer models to work out the issues. So I created a computer model of two towns on an island, sort of a modest little SimCity. I gave each town about 25,000 people, a school population, a retired population, a town budget and a property tax rate to fund it. To keep things simple, there is no inflation in this magic world, and everyone lives in identical houses. But there are a couple of key assumptions. One is that when a town accommodates to its population, it makes certain commitments: building a fire station implies a commitment to staff it, building a road creates a commitment to keep it clear of snow, and building a school implies a commitment to teach the children who attend it. These commitments are not forever, but they cannot be changed in a single year, and some of them last for several years. The other key assumption is that it takes a little while to add new capacity to the town. The demand for a new school, road or fire station has to exist for a few years before it can be accommodated.

Having set up these two little towns, they happily grow at a modest pace each on their own end of the island. The property tax rates rise a bit at first, but then stabilize nicely. (In the real world, this might correspond to the rate rising at the same rate as inflation.) All seems well, until you start moving people from one town to the other. With a set of reasonable assumptions about the sizes of the budgets and the values of the housing, migration rates as little as 1% per year can have the effect of raising taxes in *both* of the two towns. In the town losing population, the decreasing tax base has to share essentially the same level of services, and so taxes go up.[4] In the town gaining population, taxes go down for a few years, but then start rising because the taxes contributed by the new residents don't cover the costs of the services they require. Then they really spike up when the population growth levels off. A few years after you stop moving the population, the taxes settle down again, but at a higher level than if no movement had happened. Again, the only assumptions used here were that it takes time to adjust a town's capacity to fit its population, if that population changes too quickly.

---

[4]People moving from a town do leave their houses behind, but in declining towns and neighborhoods, the collection rates tend to drop dramatically.

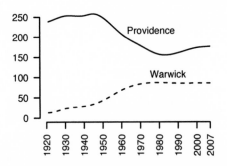

Figure 5.3: The populations of Providence and Warwick (in thousands).

This is way too simple an island to tell us much about the real world, but it does suggest that it doesn't take very much movement of people to wreak fiscal havoc. And in case anyone's forgotten, postwar Rhode Island saw migration rates many times this, as people fled Providence and the other cities in favor of the suburbs. Taxes in Providence rose quickly as the tax rolls declined, and taxes in the suburbs stayed modest only a bit longer before they, too, began to rise. The villain isn't unions. Even if union contracts are among a city's important commitments, so are buildings, bonds, and political promises to constituents. This is simply the nature of municipal government. It takes time to build capacity to serve a population, and you can't shrink it with a magic wand, either.

Providence has two-thirds the people it had fifty years ago, but it still occupies the same area, which means it still needs roughly the same number of firefighters that it had back then. The cost of those 400-odd firefighters is now borne by 175,000 people instead of 250,000. Warwick's population curve is shown in the accompanying figure. Their tax revolts began in the 1980's, when you can see population growth leveling off.

Getting back to the real island, Middletown's recent fiscal crunch came at the heels of the population decline it saw in the 1990's. Since then, growth has been modest, and that's no problem. For Portsmouth, growth is also modest, but it's leveling off after a long period of energetic growth. The situation in each town may seem the same, but the history of how they got there makes all the difference.

What this suggests is that capacity issues may be at the root of Rhode Island's property tax problems. It may simply be that in a world where moving fifteen miles isn't a big deal, towns that span only four miles may have a difficult time adjusting to changes and controlling the costs of the many services they provide.

Where did the money go?

One of the most remarkable features of debates about the state's budget crisis is that no one ever seems to talk about the fiscal effects of suburban sprawl. It sounds benign just to call it "sprawl." But if you (accurately) call it "the greatest demographic shift in our nation's history," perhaps it sounds worth accounting for.

July 2008

BECAUSE a fair amount of my time is spent detailing misconceptions about government spending, I hear this question fairly often: "Where has the money gone?" This frequently happens after people have been informed that welfare spending consitutes around 1/2 of 1% of the state's general revenue budget, or that Medicaid for the poor constitutes only around 7%. If these items that they've heard so much about aren't really the problem with government spending, then what is?

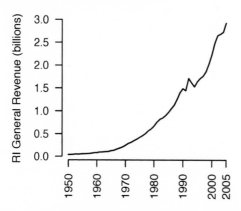

Figure 5.4: Growth of Rhode Island general revenue spending. This is dramatic growth, but it's not the only thing that's grown like this. See Figure 5.5. (Source: state budget documents, many thanks to Pat Logan at URI.)

In the winter of 2008, a friend called my attention to a fascinating set of numbers compiled by a professor at URI (see Figure 5.4, previous page). The chart showed the growth of the state budget since 1950. My friend ran across the numbers on the "Ocean State Republican" web site, where sneering comments ran like this:

> "What this data shows us is that in real terms the Democrat General Assembly has increased the State budget over NINE-FOLD since 1950! Recall that the overall population of the state hasn't changed all that much over the same exact period... Recall too that in the 1950s we already had all of the essential government services— roads, bridges, schools, water, police and fire protection— so this nine-fold increase is not attributable to 'essential government services.' "[5]

This, of course, is deeply uninformed. But let's count the ways, because they tell a good story. To begin with, population. As of the 2000 Census, there were a third more people living in Rhode Island (1.048 million) than there were in 1950 (791,000). As they say, that's not nothing.

Second, inflation. The writer used the Consumer Price Index (CPI) to correct for inflation. The CPI measures some services, like college tuitions and haircuts, but mostly it's a measure of the price of goods, and specifically goods a household buys. Households don't buy asphalt for roads, or classroom desks or judicial pensions, so already we're wondering whether this is the right index. Maybe we should use the Employment Cost Index or the Producer Price Index instead? These are all indexes of inflation, but they are all different, because inflation isn't a simple thing.

But maybe, since the whole point of the original post was to compare the cost of government to our ability to pay for it, we should look at the state's personal income. Personal income measures the size of the state's economy by how much money we all earn. In Figure 5.5 (next page), I've scaled the personal income data down and overlaid it on the general revenue spending and they track very well.

This isn't the end of the story. You can see that in 1950, the spending line is a tiny bit below the personal income data, a dif-

---

[5]*http://oceanstaterepublican.com/2008/03/27/rhode-island-citizens-one-million-boiling-frogs/*

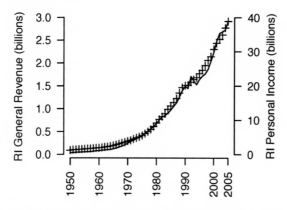

Figure 5.5: The same graph as Figure 5.4 with estimates of total state personal income plotted on top. The personal income scale is to the right. (Income estimates from Bureau of Economic Analysis.)

ference that has disappeared by 2005. This shows that general revenue has, in fact grown faster than the state's economy. Figure 5.6 shows the ratio of general revenue and personal income, which makes the change much clearer. In 1950, the government spent a tiny bit more than 3% of total personal income, while these days it's more like 7.5%.

In the web site's presentation of these numbers, they point out that in 1966, public employee unions were recognized, and in 1971 the income tax was established, and blame the acceleration on that. But that's not what this graph shows. What you see there might say that the cost rise accelerated in 1966 but whatever was going on began by 1950, or before. Public employee unions weren't around until long after this trend began. There are new state departments since then, but most of those are small ones.

So what happened? Well, how about the biggest demographic shift in our nation's history?

Fish don't notice the water

Like those clueless fish, most of us don't recognize that the world we've built around us is a very expensive one to run. Our state is filled with people ready to tell you about the positive impact of consolidating school districts and even towns. They attend school committee meetings all over the state, chanting "economies

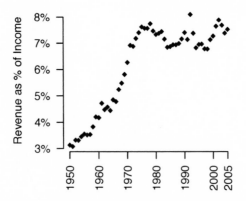

Figure 5.6: General revenue expressed as a percentage of personal income. You can see from this that we are currently spending a little more than twice what we spent in 1950. But you can also see that whatever it was that pushed us from that low level to where we are now was already well under way by 1950.

of scale" and "consolidation" and similar mantras. In my experience, though, most remain utterly oblivious to the the best way to get economies of scale: live in a city.

The truth is that moving everyone to the suburbs was a very expensive thing to do, and has cost us billions of dollars in infrastructure and operating costs, but these are costs that no one ever tots up for examination.

Here's an example: the Providence Water Supply Board provides water not only to its retail customers, who are clustered in the urban centers of Providence, Cranston and Johnston, but also to satellite water systems, which tend to be less urban, like Kent County, Warwick, Smithfield and Bristol County. In 1958, the PWSB delivered 35.7 million gallons of Scituate water each day to its retail customers.[6] In 2007, the retail customers only needed 40.3 million gallons. But the suburban systems' demand went from 4.7 million gallons in 1958 to 9 million in 1969 to 30.3 million today. All that new demand came with new miles of pipe to service, new employees to manage and new facilities to maintain. The growth was where their pipes weren't.

---

[6]1958 data from state Water Resources Board, current data from the Providence Water Supply Board, and 1969 data from a history of the Water Supply Board written in 1969 by Wayland Ingram, an engineer who worked there.

And it's not just that we've had to build new infrastructure. It's usually more expensive, too. In West Warwick, there is a sewer system, built more than a hundred years ago. It currently has a capacity of 10.5 million gallons per day, and usually operates at a bit more than half that. It uses 100 miles of sewer pipes, most of which are gravity-fed, so needs only four pumps to serve 32,000 residential customers who produce about half the sewage, and a few big industrial users like Amgen who provide the other half. Running the system costs about $9 million each year.

In 1913, when West Warwick and Warwick parted, they were two very different places. West Warwick was urban and industrial and the other rural and agrarian. Fifty years later, though, Warwick was fast losing its rural character, and in 1962, it began construction of a new sewer system. Today, the system serves around 60,000 people with 250 miles of pipe. Its total capacity is 7.7 million gallons per day, and it usually runs at around 4.5 million. Warwick is pretty flat, though, so the system has 45 pumps to move its sewage down the pipes, and it costs about $17 million each year to run it.

Warwick has a system that costs twice as much money per residential customer to run as the system in West Warwick. The reasons aren't hard to see: they have 2.5 times as much pipe and ten times as many pumps. All told, they have to spend about twice as much money each year to process *less* sewage. Meanwhile, there is enough unused capacity in the West Warwick system to service almost all the sewage Warwick produces. To put it a different way: the luxury of occupying Warwick—with its expansive 2-acre house lots and other signs of low density—costs $17 million a year in sewage processing.

The same is true of virtually any other service you can name, including gas lines, electric lines, cable TV and telephones. The cost per customer of these services in the compact urban cores is much less than the cost of providing them to customers hundreds of yards from each other. The cost of these services is borne by the ratepayers,[7] but they have an impact on other taxes, too, not merely because governments are typically the largest ratepayers for water and sewer services. We have state offices whose job it is to inspect and set standards for the water and sewer systems, and only a few of the larger systems are effectively divorced from the

---

[7]Thus, urban cable TV and phone customers subsidize the suburban ones.

management of the towns they serve. On the contrary, most share offices, vehicles, employees and bond ratings with their town governments.

Turning more directly to tax-supported expenses, how about miles of road? I found a delightful 1958 report in the state library called "Rhode Island Roads." In it, I learned that in 1958, we maintained 4,069 miles of streets and roads. By 1995, we were up to 5,893 miles, and by 2006, the mileage was at 6,528. The construction of the interstate highway system in the 1960's and 1970's obviously added miles to that sum. Because those are expensive roads to maintain and police, they added an outsize share of expense, but tremendous growth in smaller state highways and local roads are expensive, too. In 1958, we had 3,020 miles of local roads while in 2006, FHWA statistics show 5,538 miles.[8] According to DOT, resurfacing a two-lane road costs upward of $400,000 per mile.

Other expenses? According to FBI crime reports, our state has approximately 300 more police employees (officers and civilians) now than ten years ago. But these new police are concentrated in the low-crime towns that can afford them, not the high-crime places that may need them.[9] Firefighters? Providence has roughly the same number today as fifty years ago, with a third fewer people to support them, but no fewer houses to burn. Meanwhile, new fire stations have sprung up in the suburbs like dandelions on their lawns.

Schools? The story there is more complicated, and the effect of a decamping population is masked by the baby boom, changing demographics, curricula and educational norms. Despite some significant dips in the '70s and '80s, over the long term, school populations have not declined significantly in the cities, even as the overall population has. Providence, for example, now educates 23,700 children, down from around 26,000 in the 1950's, a decline of 10% in the face of a city population down by 30%. Other cities show similar stories, where the change in number of students is not what you'd expect from the raw change in popula-

---

[8]The modern data is from Federal Highway Administration reports. In the late 1980's, as GIS systems became widely used, the method of counting road miles changed. The earlier number, derived from compilation of reports from public works departments is likely not as accurate. But the purpose here is to show the scale of growth, not to calibrate it.

[9]See "It's a crime" on page 35.

tion. Pawtucket has almost the same number of students as in the 1950's, and Woonsocket significantly more. Central Falls now educates more than twice as many children as they did in the 1950's, when they were the fifth most prosperous town in the state. (Table 5.2 has these comparisons on page 91.)

In the suburbs, the enrollments have burgeoned. Porstmouth has 2,900 students, up from just 1,100 fifty years ago. North Kingstown has more than doubled its enrollment of 2,200. The increases in East Greenwich, Narragansett, and other rural and suburban towns has been even greater.

We've invested hundreds of millions of dollars in new schools since 1950. Quite a lot of that would have happened anyway, as old school buildings were improved and replaced. But the question of schools provides a fulcrum around which to turn this article from a discussion of why suburbs are more expensive to run than cities to a discussion of why, despite that, taxes are lower there.

Expensive services, low taxes

Back in the early postwar years, Providence was rich. Not just the East Side, either. There were poor neighborhoods, of course, but there was more than one rich neighborhood, as the decrepit mansions of Elmwood now testify.

A rough but decent measure of a town's ability to pay for its services is the taxable wealth behind each student in the schools. In 1950, only Narragansett, with its seaside mansions and few students, was ahead of Providence in wealth per student in its schools (see Table 5.1 on page 88). Rhode Island's other cities were right behind Providence on the list: Pawtucket, Woonsocket and Central Falls were 3,4 and 5, respectively. East Greenwich was at 29, Warwick was 33 and Hopkinton at the very bottom. The school tax rates were pretty much the exact opposite, with Hopkinton's by far the highest in the state, Warwick at number 3, East Greenwich at 11, and the top four cities and Narragansett holding down the bottom end of the list.

But then people started selling houses in the cities and buying them out of town, and property values began to shift. As early as 1959, the picture was changing. Woonsocket, Central Falls and Newport had all slid down the list. Providence and Pawtucket were still at 3 and 4, but East Greenwich had moved up to 7.

Table 5.1: Thousand dollars of assessed value per student, 1950 vs. 1993. (Source: RI Department of Education. The lists are different lengths because of district consolidations and a lack of property tax data for the Chariho district.)

	1950		**1993**
47.5	Narragansett	2823	New Shoreham
24.9	Providence	902	Little Compton
22.8	Pawtucket	800	Jamestown
22.7	Woonsocket	632	Narragansett
21.4	Central Falls	505	East Greenwich
19.5	Newport	480	Barrington
17.8	South Kingstown	419	Westerly
17.7	**RI State Average**	419	Newport
17.2	Little Compton	363	Portsmouth
16.4	Barrington	357	Scituate
16.1	Scituate	329	Smithfield
15.8	Portsmouth	325	North Kingstown
15.7	West Warwick	325	Lincoln
15.4	East Providence	320	South Kingstown
13.9	Jamestown	318	Warwick
13.7	Tiverton	314	Tiverton
13.6	Westerly	304	Johnston
13.5	Cranston	299	Cranston
13.3	Lincoln	297	North Smithfield
12.7	North Providence	280	East Providence
12.4	Charlestown	277	Middletown
11.7	Cumberland	275	Cumberland
11.6	North Kingstown	274	Bristol/Warren
11.6	Warren	273	North Providence
11.3	North Smithfield	260	**RI State Average**
11.1	Middletown	247	Foster
10.8	New Shoreham	225	Exeter/WG
10.7	Foster	206	West Warwick
10.7	Bristol	200	Glocester
10.6	East Greenwich	192	Coventry
10.5	Richmond	176	Pawtucket
10.3	Smithfield	159	Burrillville
10.1	Coventry	135	Providence
9.4	Warwick	122	Woonsocket
8.7	Burrillville	55	Central Falls
8.2	Glocester		
7.9	Exeter		
7.1	Johnston		
6.6	West Greenwich		
5.8	Hopkinton		

As the cities absorbed one hit after another to their tax rolls, they lost *some* students, but nearly enough to keep up with the revenue lost. And they didn't lose any houses to protect or streets to keep clean. They were only losing people—older people and prosperous people—and money. Meanwhile, on the other side of the coin, suburbs were gaining people whose new taxes didn't quite pay for the cost of the schools, roads and fire departments they demanded. But that was largely not a problem, because more people were coming next year, and property values were increasing, too.

During the 1960's, suburban growth rates of 4 to 5% per year were not at all uncommon (North Kingstown, East Greenwich, Coventry, among others), and they were even higher in the 1950's. When revenues are growing at more than 5% a year, anyone can balance a budget, and many did so while clucking sanctimoniously at the cities. The places that rose on the list on page 88 could finance their growth with new revenue that came in the mail, while the places that tumbled down the rankings could only moan about their lost revenue (and petition for state aid, which was only grudgingly awarded).

As late as 1977, Providence was still number 6 on this list, but the other cities had slid way down, and Providence was soon to follow. After the 1989 slump in real estate values, the list assumed its modern shape, with the cities in the basement and the rich suburbs elbowing into the company of the beach communities.[10]

The short version of all this is that the flight to the suburbs devastated our urban centers and their ability to support government services. The inexpensive government of the suburbs was only a fiction produced by astonishing growth rates and a certain lag in providing the necessary services. (For example, the obvious need for sewers in Warwick predated their construction by almost a decade.) The flight itself happened in part because of social pressures (race, poverty, desire for that little house on the 2-acre lot in the country), and in part because of consciously-chosen government policies (state support for new infrastructure, including the interstate highways, "urban renewal," funding formulas that favored growing communities, and much more).

So where has the money gone? Most of it went to build what

---

[10]The 1993 year was chosen because it was the oldest list that looked essentially similar to the situation as of 2009.

amounts to an entire second state's worth of sewer lines, police stations, roads, and schools. Union contracts, care for the poor, and increased government services are obviously an important part of the story of rising costs but the effects described here are not minor details. The expensive choices we've made have been masked by the fiscal effect of the flight to the suburbs, but that masking effect only lasts as long as the growth does. When the growth slows, that's when the piper comes for his due, and taxes rise to pay for the expenses no longer covered by growth.

The point of this observation isn't to mourn what might have been, but to make the correct diagnosis. A malignant tumor in your head may give you a headache, but you're not going to cure it with aspirin. Decapitation won't help much, either. Getting the diagnosis right isn't about exonerating anyone or blaming anyone, but about *fixing our problems*. If you don't get it right, the problems don't get fixed. You spend your time addressing the wrong issues and wonder why things don't improve—not a bad description of what goes on in our statehouse every year.

Table 5.2: School enrollments, 1954 v. 2008. An asterisk indicates a consolidated district. (Source: RI Department of Education.)

Town	1954	2008	District
Barrington	2,366	3,445	
Bristol	1,661	3,449	Bristol-Warren
Burrillville	1,293	2,586	
Central Falls	1,366	3,081	
Charlestown	350	3,644	Chariho
Coventry	1,705	5,377	
Cranston	8,866	10,684	
Cumberland	2,023	5,028	
East Greenwich	852	2,389	
East Providence	6,250	5,751	
Exeter	207	1,931	Exeter-West Greenwich
Foster	291	2,319	Foster + Glocester (total)
Glocester	508	*	
Hopkinton	836	*	
Jamestown	478	477	(HS in North Kingstown)
Johnston	2,401	3,227	
Lincoln	1,622	3,273	
Little Compton	317	313	(HS in Portsmouth)
Middletown	1,623	2,420	
Narragansett	494	1,458	
Newport	4,738	2,094	
New Shoreham	73	133	
North Kingstown	1,904	4,466	
North Providence	2,017	3,293	
North Smithfield	1,022	1,861	
Pawtucket	9,020	8,715	
Portsmouth	1,061	2,955	
Providence	26,586	23,710	
Richmond	342	*	
Scituate	822	1,713	
Smithfield	1,325	2,545	
South Kingstown	1,689	3,661	
Tiverton	1,417	1,925	
Warren	1,334	*	
Warwick	10,222	10,855	
Westerly	2,143	3,232	
West Greenwich	193	*	
West Warwick	1,956	3,556	
Woonsocket	4,029	5,955	

Six

Housing Our Hopes

Speculation speculation

Rhode Island has had a serious affordable housing shortage, and the foreclosure crisis has made it no better. But most solutions to this crisis focus on increasing the supply of housing, and not on the realities of the housing market. Here is a look at some important, and usually ignored, facts about that market, sadly still relevant, despite the cratered housing market.

January 2007

ANALYSES OF RHODE ISLAND'S real estate market are generally missing some important information. From readily available data, it's easy to see, for example, that around $5 billion of residential real estate was bought, sold, or rented in 2006. What's harder is understanding the many reasons *why* people were buying and selling. People buy property for a number of reasons. Some buy houses to live in them, others buy houses in order to re-sell them at a profit. Still others buy because their parents told them to, and there are undoubtedly sillier reasons out there, too. But does it make a difference why people buy a house? The answer is that yes it does, if you think the market isn't working well.

As of the beginning of 2007, Rhode Island had a healthy real estate market in one important respect: every seller was able to find a buyer, though they may not be able to find it at the price they want. But the reverse was not true, and hadn't been for a long time. Every buyer was *not* able to find a seller offering at a price they could afford. Depending on how you view the world, this might be a failing of the market to provide a social good (housing for everyone), or it might just be the expected functioning of the market, a necessary hardship. Whatever your economic philosophy, the fact is that the price of real estate in Rhode Island makes finding affordable housing very difficult for many, and even makes it difficult to profit by renting property. Price is an important issue, and people's motivation for buying property is part of it.

According to estimates derived from Federal Reserve investment statistics, as of 2007, around a quarter of total investment in real estate was speculative investment: purchases made not to provide a home to anyone, but in order to resell at a higher price. But this conclusion was from indirect data, obtained via gross measures of investment. Furthermore, it's national data, so the number could be much higher in pockets, since there were plenty of places in the country where the real estate bubble was far less pronounced. Better estimates can be obtained by direct measures.

For a new analysis, I obtained records of all the real estate sales in Providence in 2003, 2004, 2005 and most of 2006: 14,967 records. Of these, there were only 11,341 distinct properties. Over 3,500 of the sales were resales, on 2,778 different properties: about a quarter of all sales activity, measured in sales or in houses. About 5.5% of all sales were property flips, where the buyer held the property for less than six months.

In many neighborhoods, the number of short-term investors was even higher. In plat 43, which covers part of the West End around Cranston Street, Potters Avenue and Dexter Street, about 40% of sales between 2003 and 2006 were for rapid-fire investment, turning over at a pace 35% faster than in the rest of the city. One hundred and ninety-seven properties there changed hands during that time, but only 87 of them were involved in 220 sales.

Citywide, the average difference between purchase and sales prices for investors who held their properties for less than six months was about $60,000, or a bit more than 50% of the amount invested. From the assessor's data alone, you can't know whether this is all profit, since it's likely that the purchasers put *some* money into these properties, and this gets to the question of whether all these short-term investors are providing a social good or not. There are two common portrayals of these investors. One picture shows a population of earnest citizens, trying to do well by buying and improving pieces of the housing stock in their neighborhoods. The other picture is of rapacious minor-league land barons, making a quick buck by pumping up the value of housing for their personal benefit.

Purchase data provides a way to begin to answer the question of which picture prevails. Counting only the properties purchased and sold after the 2003 revaluation, about 11% of these short-term properties show any change in assessment between their purchase and sale. In other words, only about one investor in nine made any significant improvements to the properties they (re)sold. Others may have cleaned them up, put on a coat of paint or put in new kitchen cabinets, but nothing that shows up in the assessment. As with the other measures, though, this varies by neighborhood. In the West End's plat 43, for example, about one reseller in three made significant improvements to the property they sold.

The data also show that the property improvers are correspondingly more likely to hold the property longer. Citywide, the difference is small, with improvers tending to hold property a month or so longer (average: 11.7 months) than the non-improvers (10.5 months). In the city's poorer neighborhoods, however, the long-term improvers hold their property for the same average time as citywide, but the short-term non-improvers are more aggressive, and sell their properties three months sooner, on average.

This is consistent with other observations that lead one to believe that speculation has the greatest effect in the poorest neighborhoods. After all, houses usually have to be cheap in order to be a bargain.[1]

Another question raised by this data is how much money people are earning from these investments. The data don't make it possible to answer this precisely, because there's no way to price the coats of paint applied and because of quirks in the way multi-property sales are reported. Nonetheless, the data does support some broad observations about prices and allows rough estimates

---

[1] As an illustration, consider the case of Madeline Walker, the 81-year-old resident of South Providence whose house was lost over an $882 unpaid sewer bill in the fall of 2005. Beyond the essential unfairness of the lien laws, her case showed the pace at which real estate sales happened during the bubble. After her house was scooped up in a tax sale, it was resold twice more within only a few months (not counting the sale where one of the investors sold it to himself). Both speculators got a bargain and pocketed a tremendous profit at the expense of a poor woman who would have lost her home but for the intervention of the Governor's office (who intervened, secured legal help for her, and had the purchases nullified, putting her back in her house). Mrs. Walker's age and condition provided the public sympathy necessary to force people to act, but this kind of thing has been standard operating procedure in South Providence for years.

about profit. The first finding: it's a lot. From the data available (which doesn't count those coats of paint, remember), a conservative estimate would say that about $65 million in profit is earned each year by selling real estate in Providence that is held for four years or less. There are neighborhoods in several other Rhode Island cities and towns that match the characteristics of South Providence and Olneyville, so there is little reason to imagine that these trends aren't matched statewide, which would lead to estimates of $200-250 million per year for the whole state.

We can also see from the data that in dollar terms, approximately 21% of real estate investment in Providence is investment made for short-term gains alone. That is, 21% of the money spent on city real estate in 2003 was spent on property that was sold by 2006, and usually long before. This is a huge proportion, and doesn't count investors with a longer-term outlook. Again, projecting out to the state level, this is almost a billion dollars a year in our $4.6 billion market. This much money can only have an upward effect on prices.

Resale activity is clearly related to the level of prices. Resold property sold for 15-25% more money compared to its assessment than property that was only sold once in the study period. This is a statistically significant difference that survives analysis by the property *and* by the neighborhood. That is, houses in neighborhoods with lots of resold property sell for much more compared to their assessment than calmer neighborhoods and houses that are quickly resold sell for much more compared to their assessment than nearby houses that are not.

This analysis doesn't make it clear what is the cause and what is effect. As usual, though, it's neither the case that short-term investors cause high prices, nor is it the case that they are only passive participants, merely taking advantage of market conditions to make some money. Rather, they are an integral part of the way the market functions, for better and worse.

A land-gains tax in Vermont is a good model to discourage a great deal of the short-term investing that is so prevalent recently. The legislation contains exemptions for owner-occupied houses. As of this writing, some important details (like the tax rates) are not settled. The rates in the Vermont law range from 0%, for owners who've held their properties more than six years, to 60%, for owners who sell in under 4 months. In Vermont, this tax is not a big money-maker, and annually only raises between $400,000 and

Duration	Rate
<4 months	60%
4–8 months	35%
8–12 months	30%
1–2 years	25%
2–3 years	20%
3–4 years	15%
4–5 years	10%
5–6 years	5%
>6 years	0%

Table 6.1: The tax rates in Vermont on the capital gains from land held less than six years. These rates apply if the gains are less than 100% of the purchase price, and there are higer rates if the gains are higher.

$4 million from a real estate market approximately the same size as ours. It serves their state in a different way, by keeping their real estate market somewhat cooler than ours. Like us, Vermont is also having a crisis in affordable housing, but their housing inflation rate is less than half ours, and this tax is part of the reason why.

Our state government regulates markets in tow trucks, taxicabs, haircuts, electric rates, garbage collection, architects and insurance. The forms of regulation are all different. Some are price regulation, some regulate market entry, and others regulate conduct, or impose taxes. But they have this in common: they were all put in place because some people realized that the unfettered market wasn't serving an important social good. Our shortage of affordable housing is clearly linked to the predictable behavior of the housing market. We can decide that it's "un-American" to regulate this market, but if we do, we'll have no excuse for wondering why housing costs continue to spiral ever skywards.

A failure to plan for failures

Not only do some people fail, but they don't have the good grace to disappear afterward.

October 2008

A S THE NATION CONTINUES TO REEL from the ongoing financial crisis, the boom and bust that we're suffering, it's worth stopping to ask how it is that we got to this place.

Everyone knows that foreclosures are driving the economic crisis, but does everyone know that people falling behind in their payments isn't the big story? According to HUD statistics, in 1986, about 5.5% of all mortgages were in arrears, and about one in 21 of those went into foreclosure. In the first quarter of this year, 6.35% of all mortgages were behind in their payments, but foreclosure proceedings had begun on one in six of those. In the subprime markets, the delinquency rates are much higher (22% for variable rate mortgages), but the foreclosure rates are higher still (almost one in three). As late as 2002, the delinquency rates for this kind of mortgage were almost 15%, but only about one-sixth of the delinquent loans began foreclosures.

In other words, these are tough economic times, but at the ground level, we're not so far from other economic slowdowns. What's different now is that foreclosure is a far more likely outcome of falling behind in your mortgage payments than it has been at any time since HUD started tracking these numbers in 1986.

Why? Well, one reason might be that so many loans are held by speculators. National statistics from late 2007 (presented to Congress in January by the Mortgage Bankers Association) show that as many as a fifth of foreclosures were from investors—people who have bought property not for its rental income, but simply to resell it for a profit.

When the mortgage broker doesn't require much of a down payment, and borrowing costs are low, then anyone with persistence can make money borrowing and investing. The stakes are low and the profits high. But with the stakes so low, there is little downside to abandoning a bad buy without trying to work out terms. Even in the high-flying and now-crashing world of high finance, this has been well-known for decades, even if the rules became easy to evade in recent years.

Practically speaking, the effect of the boom in housing speculation was to annihilate what little affordable housing we have in this state. Flipping properties is not perfectly compatible with having tenants (and rents didn't keep up with sale prices anyway) so lots of housing was withdrawn from the rental market. And because the poor neighborhoods in our state are where investors could find the best bargains, those are the places now suffering most from the continuing crunch in affordable housing.[2]

But even when you discount foreclosures to investors, the foreclosure rate is high. Why? Loans sold to investors as part of mortgage-backed bonds separated the lender and borrower by thousands of miles. When the borrower gets in trouble, there's no one to appeal to for a workout. Distant companies may have all the incentive in the world to work something out, but without a local contact people can talk to, they effectively have no ability to do anything but foreclose. Democrats in Washington began calling in 2007 for action to help borrowers get workout terms where it's possible, but they've received nothing but a deaf ear until this October.[3] Seems now like it might have been a good idea, doesn't it?

But this isn't all. Lots of households are, in fact, in trouble with their mortgages, but why? If you said that they took on mortgages they couldn't afford, you'd obviously be right, but perhaps only partly right. And what do you know? The HUD statistics show an increase in foreclosures in 2006—*preceding* the rise in delinquency—but just after the Republican Congress passed bankruptcy "reform." The reform bill made it harder to enter bankruptcy, so that route out of financial trouble was shut down for millions of people, increasing the likelihood that people with troubled finances might just accept the trouble and walk away. The bill was pushed by the credit-card industry—Barack Obama voted no and is on record wanting to overturn it, John McCain voted yes, even voting against an amedment to exempt bankruptcies due to medical bills. (And yes, Joe Biden voted for it.)

We're in a slowdown that began like others, but the legal and banking deck has been stacked against individual homeowners. That's what makes me want to throw my calculator at people who

---

[2]See "Affordable housing: still missing" on page 99.

[3]And it still failed, in 2009, dying in the Democratic-led Senate. See "Why are banks in charge?" on page 26.

say this whole crisis is to be blamed on irresponsible borrowers. There's little or no evidence they've been more irresponsible than in the past, but the screws have been so tightened that more of them fail.

A hallmark of horrible public policy is a lack of concern for the failures. You see this all the time: we should close failing schools, flunk failing students, dump people off welfare who can't get a job, deny health care to immigrants (even legal immigrants). All these tough-talking policies are proposed by people who apparently imagine that the failing poor people, schools, whatever, will simply disappear. Proponents routinely deride those of us who want to accommodate the failures as softies. But here's news: they don't disappear. The people without health care overcrowd our emergency rooms, the failing students become unemployable adults, and apparently failed debtors can bring down our financial system. (Abetted, of course, by the geniuses of Wall Street.) A little more concern for the failures isn't evidence of a soft heart, but of practical minds.

Affordable housing: still missing

Despite the collapsed housing market, rents and housing costs haven't come down yet, and affordable housing is still hard to find.

December 2008

I WAS LOOKING OVER some data about homelessness in December, 2008. It seems that the number of homeless people using shelters from July 2006 to June 2007 was about the same as the year, before, which seems like good news only until you compare it to the years before that. Shelter nights in 2006-2007 were up over 70% from 2000. The most recent year's data is still being compiled, but with unemployment up and rents not down, there's no obvious reason to think things have improved.[4]

Homelessness is a complicated thing, with many reasons behind it, but high rents are a principal cause. Right now, the median rent for a one-bedroom apartment is about four times what a disabled person receiving Social Security (SSI) support receives.

---

[4]The perspective from a few months later: it didn't.

Sure, those people aren't necessarily shopping for median apartments, but show me the units that rent for $200 a month, which is about what they can afford. And that isn't the only problem.

During the crazy price run-up between 2000 and 2006 buying property in order to rent it became less and less feasible. From tax assessor data, I see that you could easily find a duplex in South Providence for between $225,000 and $280,000 in 2004. But the RI Housing rent survey from that year says that rents in the area averaged only around $750 or $800, not enough to cover a typical mortgage. The owners of these houses, where they decided to rent at all, had to push the envelope of the rental market.

According to RI Housing, the median rent in the state has gone from $750 in 2000 to $1,175 in 2006, and then down to $1,142 in 2007. Meanwhile, the cost of a median multi-family home (statewide) went from $108,000 in 2000 to $285,000 in 2006, growing almost three times as fast. The market has cratered since then, though prices still resist gravity a bit more than many had thought likely.

What's more, because many landlords were buying only to re-sell, they were not that interested in tenants, preferring to apply new paint jobs and other cosmetic work to boost resale price. Tenants tend not to make a sale easier, so apartments stayed empty pending a sale. The practical effect was to withdraw a large number of rental units from the market. Rentals were expensive *and* hard to find during the bubble years.

Of course the downside to this kind of investment is that you don't want to be holding the ball when the music stops. A lot of foreclosures in the poor parts of our state have been investors walking away from deals gone bad by falling prices, leaving what tenants they have to be evicted by the bank. In a theoretical economics sense, this *is* the market correcting itself. The problem is that the corrections appear to take some time, and the human cost is pretty high while we're waiting.

Where does this leave us? In John Steinbeck's "Grapes of Wrath," he wrote about starving farm workers watching as surplus fruit was dumped on the ground and spoiled with kerosene to keep the fruit prices from collapsing. How different is that from where we are today? A homeless person walking over to Amos House in South Providence will pass more than a handful of boarded up and vacant houses on the way.

Figuring out what to do about this is not easy. It's clear that the market isn't working to provide housing to people who need it, but the only fix policy makers in our state have been behind is to build more affordable units. This isn't a terrible idea, and the people who get to live in them are made happy, but we can't possibly build our way out of the affordable housing crisis. The available money is too small and the market is too big. Reshaping the rules that govern that market is the only way we're going to put this behind us.

When you mention the possibility of regulating the housing market, many will gasp some economics pabulum about rent control. The evidence about rent control is much more mixed than most economists would have you know, but it's controversial and difficult to make it work right, and there is quite a lot we could try besides simple price controls. For example, making it harder to withdraw rental units from the market, or offering tenants a right to stay in their homes through a sale.

A more interesting possibility would be to privilege rental income and discourage speculation income. For years, our state has cut capital gains tax rates, to encourage investment. But the kind of investment this encourages (to the extent that it encourages any at all) is the buying and selling of enterprises and real estate, not the income derived from managing them. Our state does not suffer from a shortage of savings or investable funds, as the real estate bubble itself has shown us. Capital gains tax cuts solve a problem we don't have, and create revenue problems we don't need.

Let's instead lower the tax rate on income from residential rentals and help pay for it by putting the capital gains tax rates back where they belong, equivalent to the taxes on other kinds of income. According to IRS reports, RI residents earn about $190 million in rental income each year. Cutting the income tax in half on this would cost us around $5-6 million, far less than the capital gains cuts cost us. It would also be a great idea to enact an anti-speculation land gains tax, like they have in Vermont. (See page 96.) This will barely raise any revenue at all while we're still in the dumps, but I've lived through two housing bubbles in the past 20 years, and that's quite enough for me, thank you very much. Now is the time to ensure that we don't have to go through it all again.

Seven

Is Grass Greener in Other States?

Massachusetts: The state they're in

Does anyone in Rhode Island ever take a close look at how Massachusetts does it? No, probably not.

December 2006

"Cities and towns are facing a long-term financial crunch caused by increasingly restricted and unpredictable local aid levels, constraints on ways to raise local revenue, and specific costs that are growing at rates far higher than the growth in municipal revenues.

Municipal managers and elected officials across the state—regardless of whether they live in cities, towns, resort communities and rural hamlets—understand that municipal government is nearing a crisis point. Citizens are feeling increasingly sour toward local government because their family's property tax bill has increased dramatically, they are now paying fees for many services that used to be covered by general revenue, and, still, core local government services are being cut."

SOUND FAMILIAR? It sounds like any number of recent reports about Rhode Island, but this is about Massachusetts, and is quoted from *Local Communities at Risk: Revisiting the Fiscal Partnership between the Commonwealth and Cities and Towns*, a 2005 report from the Municipal Finance Task Force, a group convened by the

Metro Area Planning Council, the umbrella planning authority for greater Boston.

During the 2005 legislative session, taxes in Massachusetts took a prominent role in conversations about Rhode Island's budget. The legislature even adopted a tax bill whose purpose was to lower taxes on the wealthiest taxpayers to levels not to exceed those in Massachusetts. The goal, apparently, was to lure rich people to live here instead of there.

Left unsaid in most of the debate last spring was what is really going on in our neighbor state. Massachusetts's economy is strong, it is a much wealthier state than ours, with a strong high-tech industry, and they were not facing any serious budget cuts this past year. So it logically follows that therefore we should achieve their success by emulating their tax policy. Right?

But as usual, policy makers in Rhode Island take only a superficial look at the factors they profess to know about, and lead us further into a disaster.

The Massachusetts budget

Massachusetts was able to balance its fiscal 2007 budget for two simple reasons. One is that the recession of 2001-2002 hit Massachusetts very hard (harder than Rhode Island who didn't have nearly as many high-tech companies to fold), and their budget that year was a debacle, with many cuts all across the board. The second reason is that since then, there has been no political will to restore those cuts, and so services that suffered in 2002 have not been restored.

Even so, and even though state tax collections in Massachusetts are up a bit in fiscal 2007, the $26 billion budget former Governor Mitt Romney signed last July is still out of balance, by at least $250 million. The budget passed last spring was only balanced by taking $550 million from the state's budget stabilization fund (the "rainy day" fund). The Governor vetoed that part of the budget, along with some $40 million in municipal funding. The legislature put the municipal funding back, but couldn't override the veto of the rainy day appropriation.

And there the matter sits. The Governor vetoed another supplemental bill in October that took only $450 million from the fund, and then slashed budgets across the board using his emergency authority. The legislature failed to override the action, and is currently holding tight, waiting for the new Governor to take office, and praying that tax collections improve.

The Massachusetts debt

Borrowing is another classic method for making a budget seem better than it is, and Massachusetts has used it freely. Not counting its counties, Massachusetts carries the highest debt per capita of any state in the nation. At $4,128 per citizen, it's close to three times the Rhode Island level of $1,402. (And it's also more than double as a percentage of personal income.) This is perhaps not a problem for them, since they are also one of the wealthiest states in the nation. Their bond rating has not suffered tremendously over it (it's a bit better than ours). But how is it that our House Finance Committee can consider their tax and budget practice a model for us? With our lower state income, if our debt level was that high, our bonds would be junk bonds.

Massachusetts cities and towns

What has suffered the most in Massachusetts is services provided by the state's cities and towns. Municipal aid was one of the big losers in the 2001-2002 budget cuts. Adding insult to injury, the legislature has added new restrictions on state aid since the recession, forcing cities to fund some services at the expense of others. Education funding has largely been maintained, but fire departments, libraries and public works departments across Massachusetts have laid people off, closed doors, and experimented with turning off streetlights. The 2005 report quoted above was compiled in response to the crisis, though it's not clear that it has provoked any significant action in the legislature.

Rhode Island is a small state, nestled in between larger and richer states. The actions we can take are obviously limited by these facts. But the fact that we are near those states does not mean that we are identical to them, and it also does not mean we can succeed by copying.

It is possible to make a case that the tax cuts in Massachusetts over the past 25 years have had a benefit to their economy. One has to ignore MIT, Harvard, and the other universities there, along with the high-tech industry concentration there to make the case convincing, but let's suppose for a moment that it is true. The evidence is pretty clear that even if some benefit accrued to the state economy as a result of the tax changes, it did not also accrue to the state budget.

To translate this into Rhode Island's terms: even if you imagine last year's tax cut for the rich to be a modest stimulus to the state's economy, you should not be fooled into thinking that this kind of stimulus will mean anything besides tighter and tighter state and municipal budgets in the future. This is "trickle-down" economics at its purest: make life better for the rich, and simply hope that the rest of us benefit.

Scandalous salaries

Rhode Island is a poorer state than either of its two neighbors, but why is that? Here's a possible answer, written in 2005, but still valid (sadly enough) today.

May 2005

IT IS VIRTUALLY AN ARTICLE OF FAITH in Rhode Island that our education costs are high because of greedy teachers and their powerful unions. Our Governor has been railing about this for some time, not without some political success, and his predecessors were not noticeably less noisy on the subject. It's true that teaching in public schools in Rhode Island is a fairly well-paid occupation. Let's trot out some of the well-worn statistics: According to the NEA—and duly reprinted by the Rhode Island Public Expenditure Council (RIPEC)—the average public school teacher in Rhode Island is paid $52.261, which is the eighth highest in the nation. This is, of course, a scandal, and the Governor (and the Assembly) use the fact as an excuse to cut funding for education. Why, after all, should they spend our precious tax dollars where they will just be absorbed by those greedy teachers?

Here in Rhode Island, this is traditionally where analysis of these situations stops. But Governors have been using the teacher unions for punching bags for many years, without successfully lowering the costs at all. You'd think that after all this yelling there would be some effect. How can it be that evil unions still dominate the finances of our towns? Could there be an alternate explanation for high salaries?

	HS Teachers		Accountants		Veterinarians	
1	NJ	62,826	NJ	56,751	NJ	78,624
2	CT	62,327	DC	54,382	CT	76,106
3	AK	60,563	AK	53,222	NV	73,307
4	PA	58,643	CT	51,618	AZ	73,258
5	CA	58,533	NY	51,247	**RI**	**72,999**
6	NY	56,914	CA	50,294	CA	72,436
7	MI	55,248	**RI**	**49,969**	NY	71,213
8	**RI**	**54,725**	HI	49,945	MD	70,600
9	DC	53,449	MA	49,063	MI	70,414
10	MD	52,377	MD	48,552	DC	70,014
	...		...		...	
49	SD	35,639	WV	39,283	MT	51,216
50	ND	34,849	SD	37,170	OK	47,663
51	MS	34,485	ND	36,704	NM	46,628

Table 7.1: Statewide average salaries. Isn't it time the Governor spoke out about the scandalously high pay of our accountants and veterinarians? (source: CareerJournal.com)

While wondering, I spent a delightful afternoon recently, clicking and copying data from *CareerJournal.com*, a service of the *Wall Street Journal*. And what do you know? It seems that our teachers are not alone in occupying a high position in salary rankings. Rhode Island hosts the nation's seventh highest-paid accountants, for example, as you can see in Table 7.1. We also have the fifth highest-paid veterinarians, the third highest-paid pharmacists, and the ninth highest-paid architects, counseling psychologists, and nurses (RNs). Perhaps, then, our high salaries are simply part of the higher cost of living in the northeast.

But then the story gets more complicated. Browsing further, I discovered that our house painters are only the 15th highest-paid in the country, and that we have the 21st highest-paid cashiers, our butchers rank 25th and our fish packers 41st. The data seemed to suggest a split between kinds of jobs, consistent enough that it seemed worth trying to quantify.

Using the list of categories on the *CareerJournal.com* site, I developed two lists of jobs. One list was for professions that seem vaguely comparable to teachers in terms of education, national average salary, and social status, and the other list was for jobs that have less of all three. Using these lists of jobs, I calculated average salaries for each state, and computed state rankings for

	Professionals		Blue-Collar			Professionals		Blue-Collar	
1	NJ	64,053	HI	33,363	26	WV	53,906	KS	25,728
2	CA	62,851	NJ	31,976	27	OH	53,878	AZ	25,445
3	CT	61,435	CT	31,310	28	WI	53,769	TN	25,396
4	MA	61,282	AK	31,191	29	FL	53,269	IA	25,294
5	DC	60,176	MA	30,045	30	IN	52,910	GA	25,153
6	MD	60,074	WA	29,357	31	MO	52,649	WY	24,968
7	NV	60,060	IL	29,168	32	NH	52,622	VT	24,708
8	**RI**	**59,720**	DE	29,094	33	UT	52,536	NE	24,635
9	AK	59,492	DC	29,004	34	ID	52,128	ID	24,611
10	NY	59,198	NV	28,868	35	MS	51,840	SC	24,333
11	MI	58,588	CA	28,705	36	AL	51,311	UT	24,299
12	DE	56,932	NY	28,516	37	ME	51,104	MT	24,161
13	IL	55,684	PA	27,711	38	SD	50,725	ME	24,075
14	AZ	55,680	OR	27,560	39	AR	50,489	LA	24,004
15	VA	55,358	MI	27,369	40	LA	49,971	NC	23,983
16	GA	55,323	MN	26,989	41	WY	49,790	KY	23,967
17	HI	55,231	CO	26,900	42	VT	49,734	SD	23,850
18	CO	55,141	MD	26,848	43	SC	49,478	ND	23,841
19	NC	54,849	IN	26,777	44	NM	49,132	OK	23,753
20	TX	54,734	OH	26,724	45	KY	48,838	TX	23,502
21	OR	54,552	NH	26,406	46	IA	48,564	FL	23,466
22	PA	54,415	MO	26,152	47	OK	48,361	WV	23,353
23	TN	54,110	**RI**	**25,994**	48	ND	48,171	NM	22,634
24	WA	54,105	VA	25,913	49	NE	48,039	AR	22,562
25	MN	54,096	WI	25,903	50	KS	47,308	AL	22,428
					51	MT	46,128	MS	22,097

Table 7.2: Professional salaries vs. blue-collar salaries: Look at how consistent the salary rank is for New Jersey, Connecticut and Massachusetts. Compare this to states like Hawaii, Washington and Iowa on the one hand, and Texas, Mississippi and Rhode Island on the other. Are professionals here paid too much or cashiers not enough?

them.[1] These are in the table above.

Some states are in roughly the same place on both lists. New York, New Jersey, Connecticut, Massachusetts all rank high on both lists. And these are widely known to be fairly expensive places to live. Louisiana and Oklahoma rank low on both lists, and these are fairly cheap places to live. So there are no mysteries there. But look at Hawaii. It ranks 17th in the list of professional salaries, but right at the top of the blue-collar salaries. Washing-

---

[1]The "professional" occupations used were Accountant, Counseling Psychologist, Clinical Psychologists, Voice Pathologist, Research Assistant, Registered Nurse, Pharmacist, Logistics Engineer, Architect, Computer Programmer, and Zoologist. The "blue-collar" occupations used were Butcher, Cashier, Cleaner, Electronic Assembly, Hair Stylist, Locksmith, Carpenter, Painter, and Fish Packer.

ton, Oregon, Vermont and New Hampshire are all similar in this respect, along with Nebraska, Iowa and Kansas. In each of these states, an architect would likely find herself with a salary lower in the national ranking than the carpenter who worked for her.

For some of these, the rural nature of the state might be a plausible explanation. Maybe the professional jobs are an urban phenomenon and the demand for clinical psychologists just isn't that big in Nebraska or Kansas. But is Hawaii rural like Iowa? Idaho is largely rural, but ranks precisely the same in both lists, so it must be more than this. Undoubtedly the explanation for any state's position in these lists is a complicated one, but it seems suggestive that many of these states have a national reputation as good places to live. If someone offered you a nursing job in Hawaii—or Seattle or Burlington—it might not need as much salary to get you to take it as it might if the job was in Coeur D'Alene.

Or Dallas or Raleigh. There are also several states that tilt the other way. These are states where the professional salaries are higher, relative to the rest of the country, than the non-professional salaries. This list is dominated by the states of the south: Texas, Florida, North Carolina, Mississippi. Of the 13 states in this group, ten are in the south, and are joined by Arizona, California and, somewhat incongruously, Rhode Island.

This survey is all about private-sector employment. These are the results of millions of employers testing the waters of their local job markets, and adjusting their salaries to result. Many of the states in the cheap-blue-collar group are not union-friendly states, and most of the hard-core industrial union states (Ohio, Indiana, Illinois, Pennsylvania) are in the cheap-professional group, which suggests that unions may have something to do with these salary differentials. But this is a much more complicated and interesting story than the simple narrative of powerful government employee unions extorting high pay from complacent municipal governments.

So what?

The essential problem seems to be that Rhode Island is, overall, a state whose income distribution is not so far from the national average, but which is nestled among some much richer states. You can see this in the graph nearby. Why this is so is a matter of debate. It could be because of Rhode Island's rich history of low-wage labor. Once upon a time, we were to Britain what North Carolina later became to us: the low-wage haven where textile jobs fled. Maybe this latter-day salary differential is a legacy of Rhode Island's early industrial policy. And maybe not. Maybe it's just because Rhode Island is, due to its size, more urban a place than the whole of Massachusetts or Connecticut. Trying to tease out the threads of causation in something as complex as income distribution is a difficult task. The analysis here doesn't pretend to have the answer. But it *is* a complicated question, and people who pretend otherwise aren't really interested in solving real problems.

But here's one thing we learn: Many people in Rhode Island— including most of the folks in office these days—look at the picture in Figure 7.1 (next page) and say we're a poor state because we are chasing our rich people away, and therefore we have to cut their taxes, and mow their lawns and offer them backrubs. But the evidence from the *Wall Street Journal* is that it might be the other way around. Perhaps we are a poor state relative to our neighbors because the blue-collar jobs around here don't pay as well as they do in neighboring states.

Professional jobs are good jobs. People are often willing to move quite a distance to take a position in an architecture firm or psychology practice. People looking for such work are likely to apply for jobs far from their homes, and move if they are successful. If they don't want to move, people commute, often long distances, for rewarding and lucrative work. It's not uncommon to find software engineers who commute to the Boston area from Rhode Island because the pay is better.[2] For jobs in this category, Providence is in essentially the same job market as Boston or New Haven, or Sharon or Stonington. Like any employer, if the state wants to hire qualified architects, it has to advertise for those positions at a salary level that will attract qualified applicants who may well be considering other positions in other states.

Being a cashier, on the other hand, is not a job most people would relocate for. The job market for this kind of work is much more local. It's easier for employers to resist the pressures of higher pay in other places, since the people who might fill those jobs aren't as mobile, often due to poverty, or aren't willing to

---

[2]And many others. The parking lot for the commuter trains to Boston fill up by 7:15, and it's not cashiers making the hour-long commute.

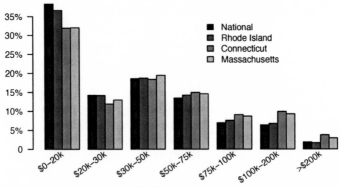

Figure 7.1: Distribution of AGI. The vertical axis shows the proportion of tax filers in the given income range. Rhode Island is at or slightly better than the national average for the most part, but Connecticut and Massachusetts are, on the whole, richer states, with smaller proportions of poor people and higher proportions of rich ones. (Source: IRS Statistics of Income reports)

commute so far for a job like that.

So here's an answer for how to deal with the high salaries earned by our teachers: raise the minimum wage. Have the state and every municipality enact and enforce living-wage legislation, where every government contract is given with the stipulation that the jobs created will be jobs that pay a living wage. Demand that large employers provide health coverage to their employees. Because we are such a small state, we may not be able to have much effect on the region, but there are a number of things Rhode Island can do to affect the local job market to push up wages to parity with our neighbors. Our policy makers always claim to be worried about parity with Massachusetts and Connecticut. Well here's a place to put their money where their mouths are.

It must be clear by now that it's worth being very skeptical of interstate comparisons and rankings. For one thing, it's not at all obvious why anyone should think that South Dakota and Rhode Island are comparable in what it takes to attract and retain a good teacher. But this is what rankings implicitly assume. Some interstate comparisons are enlightening, but hardly all. State boundaries are arbitrary products of history, not facts of nature. So what is the right level of pay for teachers? How about whatever it takes to attract and keep qualified and talented teachers? Is the amount we pay too high? Too low? Don't rely on state rankings. Go ask your local principal whether your school district's ads get responses from good candidates. If you're concerned about the quality of education, that's the only measure worth taking.

In the end, we can't change our location. Rhode Island is situated between Massachusetts and Connecticut, whether we like it or not. Unlike, say, Hawaii, the market for jobs to be filled by relatively mobile people will always have to take our neighboring states into account. Where it had to do so, the private sector has accommodated itself to this fact, as shown by *CareerJournal.com*. School departments around the state appear to have made almost exactly the same decisions about the job market as thousands of private employers in Rhode Island. It seems odd to blame them for this.

Instead of casting aspersions, the state could help, not by attempting to deny the reality of our geography, but by working to improve the situation of the people at the lower end of the employment ladder. We can have an effect on that job market, since the people in it are largely less mobile. We can't change the hand we're dealt, but we can certainly try to play it better.

New Hampshire: Our flinty neighbors to the north

We hear a great deal about New Hampshire while debating taxes in Rhode Island. But little of it is informed by the details of that state's situation, which is more than slightly different than the superficial picture that always appears when conversations turn to taxes.

October 2007

BROADCAST TELEVISION has made our nation more homogeneous, but it hasn't erased all the differences yet. Talk to anyone who has recently moved to another state and you'll find a long list of little things that are done differently there. A friend moved to Virginia recently and was pleasantly surprised to discover the extensive network of community swimming pools and the swim teams that inhabit them, something Rhode Island doesn't really have. (On the other hand, time at an ice rink is pretty hard to find there.)

Often, the differences are masked by the similarity. We have high-school football games, and Texans have high-school football games. But the scale of the enterprise is entirely different, and if you don't inquire for the details, you miss the whole story. Which brings us to some missing details about New Hampshire.

I spent a little while recently talking to people about government services in the Granite State. Since Rhode Island, for the most part, takes up very little psychic room there, the people I spoke to were a bit surprised to learn how much we hear about their state. But without a sales tax or an income tax, they are the low-cost alternative to Boston, and have done well by that strategy. There are plenty who believe that we should learn from this example, and they rarely seem shy about saying so. A September, 2007, letter in the *Providence Journal* pointed out that New Hampshire maintains four times the road mileage as we do, and they do it without an income tax. A September 19 op-ed echoed the same. A story in the October 4 *Journal*, about *Inc.* magazine's two-star rating of Governor Carcieri's record has advice from *Inc.*'s publisher that we would have had some of New Hampshire's job growth if we had a similarly "favorable tax climate." The list goes on.

But these articles overstate the case. According to the 2002 census of state and local governments, New Hampshire and its counties and towns raised about $5.1 billion in taxes, while Rhode Island and its towns raised about $4.8 billion. We divided our taxes among about a million people, and they among 1.25 million. So, per person, their taxes work out to about 89% of ours: New Hampshire may be a low-tax state, but it's sure not a no-tax state, which is the image that many people around here seem to have.

Still, 11% lower taxes isn't anything to sneeze at. How do they do it? Mostly, it turns out, by simply not providing services we take for granted here, or by providing them through property-tax-funded towns and counties. Here's an entirely random and non-exhaustive list of some food for thought:

Corrections ~ New Hampshire counties (supported by county property taxes) run jails for short-term offenders, and run the county court system. These are state functions here.

Welfare ~ Towns in New Hampshire play an integral part in the provision of the "safety net" for poor residents. Welfare directors in each town are responsible for providing whatever help is necessary—out of town budgets—to "any person who is poor." In Rhode Island, we have welfare directors, but in most towns the office merely directs applicants to private or state agencies that actually provide help, or coordinates charitable efforts on behalf of the poor.

Tuitions ~ Funding for Rhode Island's state colleges has slowed, and tuitions have gone up by a lot, but we still aren't at New Hampshire's level. A year's tuition at the University of New Hampshire costs over $10,400 compared to $7,700 at the University of Rhode Island. A semester at CCRI costs $1,100, but New Hampshire community colleges are over $1,900.

Libraries ~ New Hampshire has town libraries, and Rhode Island has town libraries. But, unlike New Hampshire, a significant portion of our libraries' funding comes from the state, which also contributes to the maintenance of a common card catalog, and to a cooperative network where each library extends borrowing privileges to the patrons of all the others.

Planning ~ New Hampshire has essentially no statewide or regional planning capacity. Towns are pretty much on their own. Rhode Island has a comprehensive planning statute that is a national model, and though there are glitches in the process, the state does take a careful look at municipal "Comp" plans and tries to ensure that a town's plans don't conflict with the policy of the state or with its neighbors. In New Hampshire, they let the courts work this out.

Education ~ Leaving aside the question of funding levels for public education in the two states, New Hampshire's Department of Education does not provide some important services that we take for granted here. Rhode Island's Info-Works, SALT and In$ite programs all provide valuable information on the achievement and spending of our local school districts in a way that allows good comparisons between them. Nothing like them is available in New Hampshire.

Health ~ Many of the functions of the Rhode Island state health department—epidemiology, public health, food inspection—are, in New Hampshire, the responsibility of the towns (if anyone).

The tax comparison itself also has interesting wrinkles. If I, a self-employed individual, were to move to low-tax New Hampshire, my state taxes could *increase*. New Hampshire imposes an 8.5% tax on "business profits," and the businesses in question are defined much more broadly than in Rhode Island. (They have triple the number of corporate taxpayers, but only 20% more people.) The business owner is allowed to be paid an untaxed "reasonable" wage, but the rest is taxed. For businesses that earn more than $150,000 per year, the tax rises to 9.25% of income. These are quite high rates compared to other states, and with very few exemptions, these taxes fund almost a quarter of their budget. By comparison, Rhode Island's corporate taxes fund only 4% of our budget and are so riddled with exemptions and credits that 94% of businesses only pay the minimum.

New Hampshire also assesses a 5% tax on interest and dividend income, which is a *higher* tax than Rhode Island assesses on this kind of income, for all except people who earn more than around $120,000 a year. So business owners and retirees often pay more than they do here. No one is going to dispute that taxes are, on the whole, lower in New Hampshire than in Rhode Island, but as usual, the picture is not as simple as it's made out to be, and the people who insist on the simple-minded comparisons are doing more to obscure the issues than reveal them.

What about the property tax? They have lots of towns, and some tax high and some are low. But it's quite easy to find New Hampshire towns where the tax rate is much higher than in any town here. Most of those are the places where the residents outnumber the tourists. Like several of our seashore towns, a lot of New Hampshire belongs to out-of-state owners. When out-of-towners are paying the bills, taxes can be lower, because people whose real homes are elsewhere also educate their children elsewhere, and they don't call the police in the off-season either. We see the effect here, too, which is why Block Island, Little Compton, and Narragansett have low tax rates. So Franconia and Jackson, up in the mountains, have very low rates, while towns like Keene and Jaffrey, in the unfashionable parts of the south, have rates double or triple those.

Another big difference is clear when you look into the facts. New Hampshire's social spending is lower in large part because it's a richer state; income is higher and the poverty rate is about half what it is here. Some will say that's because of their low taxes and pro-business "climate". But urban poverty has been a source of trouble for decades, and even back when the two states had roughly equal average incomes, poverty was much higher here, because we've got cities, and they don't. (Manchester, their biggest city, is just a bit bigger than Warwick.) In 1980, the poverty rate was 10.7% here and only 7% there, but the per capita incomes in both states were about $9,200. We had more poor people, but apparently we had more rich people, too.

So why are the states so different? The reason one place grows to regard as normal what another place thinks of as extreme is one of those mysteries that make our world a fascinating place, but there are some obvious differences in geography that seem relevant. Both New Hampshire and Rhode Island abut Massachusetts, a state whose economy, driven by its universities, has been one of the more remarkable success stories of the last few decades. But New Hampshire's border was mostly wide-open rural areas ready to become suburban developments (for better or worse) while much of Rhode Island's border was already occupied by cities. As the interstate highways allowed people to flee cities over the past 40 years, New Hampshire gained and Rhode Island lost, for no reason other than geography. I-93 brought people *to* rural New Hampshire and I-95 took people *from* Providence.

Heaven knows we don't run our state government very efficiently. Sometimes comparisons with other states can be revealing, but more often what they show is the limitations of such comparisons. New Hampshire is a very different place than Rhode Island. To the credit of its government, they've been able to capitalize on their advantages to prosper over the past two decades. I wish we could agree to capitalize on our own advantages, rather than just wish we had theirs.

Eight

Fun With Statistics

Census numbers: What do they mean?

Each December, the Census Bureau publishes updates to the American Community Survey. This gives estimates of population changes over the previous year for each state. A shrinking population isn't necessarily the end of the world, but in an economic sense, it makes it harder to grow an economy.

RIGHT BEFORE CHRISTMAS, the Census Bureau published its estimates for state population changes as of July 2008. The news wasn't great for Rhode Island, which is along with Michigan, one of only two states to lose population between 2007 and 2008. You can bet that this will provoke the usual round of teeth-gnashing, and since most of the usual teeth-gnashers find everything to be a reason to cut taxes on rich people, you can bet that's coming, too.

But what is the story behind these numbers? Is it worth inquiring further about what they really mean? Your answer to this question will depends on whether you really want to solve problems, or whether you just enjoy complaining about stuff. I am interested in solutions, so I peeked, and this is some of what I found.

The first thing worth noting is that our population decline is *less* than it was last year. We lost a lot of people in 2005, but things have been getting better since then. This is the opposite of the case in Michigan, whose population loss is getting worse. By itself this isn't necessarily cause for comfort, but it does mean that whatever is going on here is probably not the same thing as is going on in Michigan. Undoubtedly a part of the problem is the lack of jobs here, and our unemployment rate rivals Michigans for national honors. But the population drop was greater last year, when the unemployment rate was much lower, so that's not really a satisfying explanation.

So, it seemed worth turning over some rocks. I looked some at the components of the changes: births, deaths, migration. One interesting thing is that our "natural" growth rate (that is, not counting migration) is lower than many other places. For example, in 2007 we had 12 births per thousand people and so did the metropolitan Boston area. But they only had 7.8 deaths per thousand people, while we had 9.3. Ours is an older population than in many other states.

Isn't this just an unimportant detail? No. Look at Connecticut's Fairfield County, which contains Bridgeport, one of the poorest places in New England, but also Westport, one of the richest in the country. Fairfield has only about 12% fewer people than our whole state. For every thousand people in Fairfield in 2007, 10.5 left for another place in the US, while 9.5 left here. But Fairfield's death rate is much lower, and they get more immigration from other countries, so they're holding steady in overall population.

At this point, I thought to myself, these numbers are only estimates. The Census statisticians are good at their jobs, and I'm not going to contradict them, but we have some real numbers, too. I recently saw a table of Rhode Island district school enrollments over the past five years, and those numbers are even more unsettling. With the exception of Barrington, all of our school districts have lost students since 2004. Some districts have lost more than 10% of their students over that time. South Kingstown and Providence have lost 12% and Newport has lost 21%.

Declining school populations reveal that the Census estimates are probably right, and since we seem to be losing a higher percentage of students, it's likely that the departing population is a lot of families with children.

School enrollment data, because it's sorted by town, give us a way to probe for possible causes. I tried correlating the losses with other kinds of survey data about our towns, and wasted an afternoon testing variables like median incomes, per capita incomes, proportion of renters to owners and so on. The best correlation I found was with the ratio of average rents to income. The higher the average rent as a proportion of the average income, the more likely a district is to see enrollment losses. In other words, the more expensive the housing in a town, the more likely those schools are to have fewer kids today than in 2004. Our population loss is as likely to be an affordable housing issue as it is anything else.

None of this is to say these numbers are not very worrisome. Declining populations have real consequences for government services, and the most important consequence is that the cost of the services we provide goes down slower than the number of people they're provided for. It's sort of a reverse effect to economies of scale. It costs just as much to educate 20 kids as it does to educate 25, because you still need a teacher and a building and heat for the classroom and so on. Losing five kids does not mean you can cut five kids' worth of education funding, even if the state and lots of town councils try to manage things that way.

So what do we do about this? Right at the moment, of course, we can't really build much housing because of the fiscal handcuffs our leaders have put on. But building our way out of the affordable housing problem has never been a good option. We can address the housing market in a useful way—with laws about housing speculation, and rules to preserve rental units and favoring rental income over capital gains. Addressing the real pressures on municipal budgets would help, too, since property taxes are a big part of rents. We must acknowledge that affordable housing *is* an economic development issue. You want jobs here? We need places for people to live where you don't have to go broke just to pay the rent.

Goin' places

*In 2009, the Greater Providence Chamber of Commerce claimed in
a press release that IRS statistics showed that Rhode Island is losing millions in income due to migration. This is a bizarre misread
of the IRS migration data, but there are some interesting things
to be learned from that data nonetheless. This article from a year
earlier anticipated some of their claims.*

February 2008

A S THE ASSEMBLY DEBATES tax policy this year, once again the
issue of moving rich people has arisen. The fear is that "raising" taxes on the very wealthy will cause a mass exodus. Never
mind, of course, that we're in year three of a multi-year tax cut for
those same people.

It turns out that where people move to is also a subject of some
interest to the IRS, which publishes migration reports for states
every year. Shocking, you say, there's actual data? Come, tell me
if it's true: Are rich people leaving our state?

Indeed, the data do not lie: they are leaving, by the thousands.
Of course, the data also show us that other rich people are *coming*
to the state, also by the thousands. There is no denying the trou-
blesome news for Rhode Island in these reports, but it's certainly
not what you hear on a typical afternoon on WHJJ.

I bought five years' worth of this data, for years between 1989
and 2006. Each year, the data show the number of tax returns
filed by people who arrived here, and what state they came from,
the number who departed, and where they went. There are also
estimates of the income earned by the migrants in their new state.
Like all data sets, there are some limitations, most obviously that
this only applies to people who file tax returns.

That said, what do we see? The most interesting, and highest volume, exchange is with Massachusetts. In 2006, 4,538 families (7,614 exemptions, most of which are people) moved from
Rhode Island to Massachusetts, where they collectively earned
about $218 million. That same year, 4,199 taxpayers (6,679 peo-
ple) moved the other direction, and they earned $196 million here.
Net, we're down 339 taxpayers (and their families, where they
have any). So who are all these people? These data don't have
a lot to tell us, but we can say that both groups have fewer children, and earn less, on average, than Rhode Islanders who stayed

behind. The departures earn a bit more than the arrivals, but it's quite close ($48,100 vs. $46,800). To me, the small number of dependents and the respectable-but-modest mean incomes sounds most like the movement of young professionals, looking for better work.

Five years earlier, the story was different. That year, only 3,825 people left here for Massachusetts, while 4,708 moved the other way. The average income of the arrivals that year was significantly higher than the departures, too. (Though again, neither was as high as the incomes of people who stayed put.) Of course, that was the year that the high-tech industry in Massachusetts really tanked. The jobless rate was much lower here. Before that, in 1997, when the jobless rate was the other way around, the flow was the other way around, too.

The measures of income in this data can be misleading, since you can't tell whether this is income a migrant takes with him or her. That is, someone moving to another state might be taking their income with them, if it's a pension or investment income, or moving in order to take a job in that state. Both cases would look the same in these data, so it is simply *wrong* to read this data as a loss of income from one state or another.

Nonetheless, I learned something from how the incomes flow. Take Florida as our second example. There is a significant difference between the low incomes of the 984 taxpayers who moved here from Florida and the 2,529 who moved the other way. Again, however, the incomes of the leavers are, on average, lower than that of the people who stay. Doubtless plenty of wealthy people move to the Sunshine State. But for every rich migrant who earns $200,000, there are apparently 15 families in the $44,000 range making the same trek, leaving the mean a bit less than $54,000.

Several states send us rich people. New Jersey, Maryland, and Ohio seem to be major sources of wealthy people. (Along with Connecticut and Virginia, until 2004-2005.) Migrants from those states have incomes substantially higher than the incomes of people already here. Except for New Jersey, the 2006 flow of people is from Rhode Island to these states, but apparently we're getting wealthier taxpayers than we send them in exchange.

One of the troubling signs apparent in these data is a loss of children. The Pied Piper apparently marches south from here, and you can see a fairly large loss of families with children, mostly to the south (except Florida). The incomes of the departures to and arrivals from southern states are all lower than the incomes of stayers, but the net flow of children is clearly south.

To be quite clear, this data isn't detailed enough to do anything more than suggest what's going on.[1] It doesn't tell us exactly who is doing the moving, or why. The broad pattern is essentially the same as we learn from Census data. Rhode Island is losing population, and has been since economic conditions in the rest of the country improved in 2003-2004. Families with children seem to find life congenial in the south; people with average incomes and few children frequently move to Florida; single people find opportunities elsewhere, but especially California, Washington, Oregon and New York. Meanwhile, relatively wealthy folks from New Jersey, Connecticut, Maryland and Virginia seem to find life satisfying here. None of this is particularly earthshaking news.

Though the data can only suggest what *is* going on, it can be much clearer about what *isn't*. You can't exactly tell who's coming and going, or whether they're taking income with them or moving for a new job. But you can tell that wealth is mostly staying put. The mean income of departures is much lower than those who stay, both overall as well as for all but a small handful of direct comparisons. The only two of those that receive appreciable numbers of Rhode Islanders are Illinois and Ohio, where the traffic is less than 200 taxpayers in either direction.

It would be very challenging to use this data to support a theory that wealth is flowing from Rhode Island, except inasmuch as it flows with people seeking their as-yet-unrealized fortunes elsewhere. Those people are our future, so cannot be ignored, but to imagine that tax changes to favor wealthy people are the only, or even the best, solution, is only fantasy. A healthy economy requires investors, certainly, but it also requires workers, infrastructure, educational opportunity, markets and much more. To focus state policy solely on investors at the expense of the rest, as we have done and are doing, is to miss most of the picture of what makes a healthy economy, and will only drive more young people to look for opportunity in other states.

---

[1]To be specific it certainly doesn't show that wealth is moving out of state, as fevered press releases from the Chamber of Commerce have claimed. If a recent college graduate moves to Boston to take a $40,000 job, these data will show a migration of someone with a $40,000 income. To claim this is a "loss" of $40,000 to the Rhode Island economy is absurd.

Measuring teacher quality

This article limns a dispute about teacher quality statistics raised about a 2006 report I wrote. The dispute itself is fortunately forgotten, but the article is a decent explanation of some important statistical points that teach us how to read statistical results.

August 2006

IN MAY OF 2006, Working Rhode Island, a coalition of the state's largest unions, including the two teacher unions, released a report about education, *The Shape of the Starting Line*, written by the editor of this august journal, me.[2] In an op-ed in the *Providence Journal* (July 16), Valerie Forti, the director of an organization called the Education Partnership, had quite a few less-than-kind things to say about the report. She accused the report "authors" of "cherry-picking" and intellectual dishonesty for omitting some important data about teacher quality.[3] But it's worth some column-inches to explore one of the topics she brought up: teacher quality. Forti took me to task for not including the findings of Linda Darling-Hammond, an education researcher at Stanford University, whose research—according to Forti—shows that:

> "... the percentage of well-qualified teachers in a district is typically 2.5 to 3 times more important than student poverty in its net impact on student achievement."

This is a strong claim. Unfortunately, it's not supported by other studies. In fact, it's not even supported by the Darling-Hammond study she cites.

It's impossible to be serious about educational reform without considering teacher quality. It's an undeniable fact that some teachers are better than others, and discussions of certification standards, professional development, attrition, pay scales and more are all associated with this fact. The *Starting Line* does contain a discussion of teacher quality, citing work by economists Eric

---

[2]This is available at *http://whatcheer.net/ripr/wri-startline.pdf*.

[3]She also complained the report omitted important data about the effects of unions on education. In fact, there was a discussion that cited four references supporting the very point she accuses me of "conveniently" omitting. Being charitable, one might point out that there were literally dozens of pages in the report, and the executive summary was not exhaustive. You can find a link to the op-ed, as well as a reply, by searching on "Forti" at *http://whatcheer.net*.

Hanushek (also at Stanford), John Kain and Steven Rivkin and the team of William Sanders and June Rivers, of the University of Tennessee.[4]

Hanushek's study was an analysis of data from the Harvard/UTD Texas Schools project. This study collected data from 3,000 schools on half a million students from grades 3-6 between 1993 and 1995, along with a great deal of data about the teachers in the system. Because the data include multiple measurements of the same children, they could identify classrooms that did a good job at raising the achievement of their students, and then look at those classrooms and see what characteristics correlated with success. What they found was that class size effects were significant for poor children, not so much for affluent ones, and one or two years of experience for the teacher makes a difference, too. But they also found that there were large disparities in performance among classrooms that could not be easily explained by obvious factors like graduate degrees or years of experience, and there is nowhere else to credit those differences except to the teacher.

The Sanders study was along similar lines, but included more detail in the data. The Tennessee data they used followed a cohort of urban students as they progressed from grades 2 to grade 5. The researchers used the data to determine which classrooms were the most effective, and then they compared the students who had been in three effective classrooms in a row with the students who had seen three ineffective classrooms in a row. At the end of three years, the difference between the groups was as much as 50 percentiles, even after controlling for student differences. This is a huge difference—the authors use exclamation points for it.

Both these studies are about improvements in achievement, not achievement levels themselves. Their findings cannot be taken to contradict other research that describes the importance of poverty in determining academic outcomes.[5] But neither study leaves any doubt that teacher quality is very important. The beauty of the approach of these studies is that they overcome

---

[4]Citations to the Hanushek and Sanders papers can be found in the *Starting Line* report. The Darling-Hammond paper can be found at *http://epaa.asu.edu/epaa/v8n1/*.

[5]Even if you could wave a magic wand and make all Rhode Island's teachers uniformly excellent, poor kids would still start first grade behind wealthier kids in school, so the urban schools would likely still "underperform" relative to their more affluent suburban counterparts.

the major difficulty in assessing the effects of teacher quality: measuring it.

Measuring quality

It's one thing to say that teacher quality is important. It's an entirely different thing to figure out what that really means. Many of us had good teachers as children. But how would you define the goodness of those teachers? A teacher who is smart, perceptive, caring, attentive, imaginative and kind is a fine thing, but how on earth do you measure that? A principal doesn't really need to measure it; you don't need to get a precise measurement to find such teachers and keep them. But educational researchers who want to know how *much* teacher quality matters need to measure it, and this is the real Achilles' heel of this kind of study. Hanushek's and Sanders's studies overcame this, but many other studies do not.

The 2000 Darling-Hammond study is intended to show the value of teacher education and certification, so does not try to elide the issue. In fact, finding and describing just such correlation appears to be the defining argument of Linda Darling-Hammond's career, and her 2000 study is devoted to demonstrating that states would do well to raise education requirements for teachers.[6]

The support for the claim about poverty vs. teacher quality comes from Table 3 in the report, where Darling-Hammond lists correlation measurements for educational outcomes and different factors. There are estimates for teacher quality, of course, and also for poverty. The teacher quality numbers are roughly three times as great as the poverty measurements, *ergo* three times as important. But here's the problem: this is state-level data, presented as a guide to policymakers at the state level. The data used here are statewide averages—test scores, incomes and teacher degrees. The message of this study is meant to be something like "Hey Governor, you should raise professional teaching standards in your state because it's an easy route to improving the outcomes of your state's schools." As a guide to policy, this is important news to governors. But it's not a guide to the outcomes to expect in any classroom.

---

[6]The Hanushek study looked at this, and found no correlation between teachers with an advanced degree and effectiveness, but his analysis is different than Darling-Hammond's, who looked at different kinds of degrees and certification requirements.

The problem is in the confidence intervals.[7] The correlation for Darling-Hammond's measure of teacher quality has a very small confidence interval. This means it's a number to be trusted and would likely come out the same in another study. But the confidence interval for poverty is quite large, and in fact the numbers presented there are either not statistically significant, or just barely so. The reason for this is obvious: the income range *within* a state is as high or higher than the range *among* states. Greenwich, Connecticut is as rich a place as any in the country, and Bridgeport is as poor. But Connecticut's place in the income ranking in this study is represented by just one number.

What this means is that it is simply incorrect to think you're getting anything useful by dividing the number Darling-Hammond provides for the importance of teacher quality and the number she provides for the importance of poverty. One is a reliable number and one is not. That's why she provides the confidence intervals in the table: so you can tell the difference. In the world of statistics, unreliability is contagious. The result of a calculation made with an unreliable number is unreliable, no matter what else goes into it. In a statistical sense, the "2.5 to 3" cited in Forti's article has no meaning.

Darling-Hammond says, in the same paper:

> "In particular, the size of relationships found between variables measured at the state level cannot be assumed to represent the effect sizes one would find in a classroom level analysis."

---

[7]"Confidence" in statistics is another of those intimidating concepts that, under the hood, turns out to be pretty obvious. Say I have ten worms to measure and I measure the first nine and get these numbers:

$$(4, 3, 2, 1, 5, 6, 8, 7, 9)$$

The average value is five inches, but I'm not really going to be very sure that number ten will be five inches long. But if my first nine measurements are these:

$$(5, 5, 5, 5, 5, 5, 5, 5, 5)$$

The average is *also* five, but more important, I'll be fairly confident that the tenth worm will measure five inches. I might be wrong, but I'll have a right to be surprised. In the first case, I have no right to be surprised. The averages are the same, but the meaning of the average isn't. Confidence intervals are just a number that stands for this additional meaning. A wide confidence interval means that the number may just be some kind of statistical fluke, and another measurement is unlikely to give the same result, so you can't base too much on it. A tight confidence interval means that the number is easily repeated and the next time you make a measurement it will be likely to come out the same.

This is typically delphic in that academic-paper kind of way, but what she means is that the work published is meant as a broad guide to state policies, but not a precise diagnosis of what is most important for the education of an individual child. To use this data to make the kind of statement that Forti does is to completely miss the point.

Darling-Hammond's work, including her 2000 study, contains some useful guides to policy. She does point out that over the last two decades, Connecticut, Kentucky and North Carolina made impressive leaps forward in student achievement by focusing state policy on improving the quality of the teachers who teach in their schools. She does show that these efforts are likely to bear riper fruit than reductions in class size and simple raises in teacher salaries.[8] But she doesn't show that teacher quality is "more important" than poverty.

The humor in all this is that the studies that are cited in the *Starting Line* report make essentially the same case that Forti wants to make, and do it in a much more intellectually sound way than she chooses. Eric Hanushek is one of the more persuasive advocates for improving teacher quality, and the Sanders and Rivers results are about as dramatic as anything can be in the world of statistical studies of education. Exclamation points don't come cheap in academia. Does this mean that poverty doesn't matter when you're talking about the education of children? Of course not.

Hanushek's and Sander's results do imply that a few successive years of study with good teachers is enough to overcome the deficit of starting poor, but again, this is a statistical statement about classroom-level achievement, and its relation to real possibilities is tricky. Given how much snow I can move in a day's work, in theory I could build a tremendous snow fort in a year. But it's not just up to me and my ability. The weather has something to say about it, too: snow doesn't last that long around here. And you could do tremendous things with great teachers, but it's not just up to them.

Children are not mere sponges that sit where you put them and soak up lessons. The world's finest teachers buy you no advantage if the kids in those classrooms have undiagnosed vision prob-

---

[8]Those states' reforms involved increasing salaries, but the increases tended to be targeted at cities that found it hard to compete in the job market, and also involved increases in certification requirements, revamping teacher education and professional development programs, and more.

lems, if they can't stay a whole school year because their family can't find a place to live, if they are too hungry to concentrate on lessons, or if their home environment won't let them read peacefully. Findings from research about these factors are every bit as statistically solid as the findings about teacher quality.[9] These data don't conflict at all, and to think that they do only reveals a misunderstanding of what survey methods can tell us about the world.

The real lesson in Forti's op-ed is an important one about public policy debates. Many people—and she appears to be one—participate in such debates assuming that they can only be right if everyone else is wrong. But it's a complex world, and survey questions and statistical methods that condense the reality of thousands of individual teachers and children into a few numbers can only describe that reality, well, through a glass darkly. Surely there are ways to design a study to say whether poverty has a bigger impact than teacher quality, but the studies discussed here aren't them. They have other useful lessons to teach us, about how to improve teaching, and we'd be fools to ignore them just to score debate points.

Statistically speaking

A lot of conversation about state budget and tax issues depends on the misuse and misunderstanding of some important statistics. Mark Twain notwithstanding, not all statistics are lies, but it usually takes some peeking to understand them properly. The danger is especially dire when the statistic seems to confirm conventional wisdom. Artemus Ward (or maybe Mark Twain or Ralph Waldo Emerson) put it: "It ain't so much the things we don't know that get us in trouble. It's the things we know that ain't so."

March 2006

WHAT DOES A STATISTIC *mean*? Any statistic is just a measurement of some quantity. But a measurement rarely tells you anything definitive without the context. Knowing that the average height of the students in some school is 66 inches means something very different if we know that it's a college or an elementary

---

[9]And they are also outlined in the report that sparked this dispute.

school. If it's a college, it means that the boys are tall, unless it's an all-male school, in which case they're a bit below average. (See Figure 8.1 on page 131.)

In other words, a number by itself means nothing at all. The meaning only comes when it is presented along with other numbers and the argument why it means what the presenter says it does. But everyone knows this. Children know this.

"Look, I'm five foot ten inches," I say.

"You're wearing shoes with heels, Daddy," comes the reply.

Simple stuff, but somehow this critical facility is lost in many when presented with scientific sounding data. Here are three examples seen regularly:

- Only 1.86% of Rhode Island residents earn more than $200,000 per year, while the corresponding number in Massachusetts is 3.06%.

- Rhode Island teachers are paid a higher proportion of the state median wage than in any other state in the country.

- The state spent $663 million in state tax dollars on social services in 1996, and $1.233 billion in 2006.

In each case, the measurement is typically interpreted in only one way. But let's look at each of these in turn.

Those missing rich people

Critics of Rhode Island's tax policy have made much out of a comparison between the number of taxpayers who earn more than $200,000 per year in Massachusetts and Rhode Island. In tax year 2003, 3.06% of Massachusetts residents reported gross income over $200,000, while only 1.86% of Rhode Islanders are similarly blessed. The critics claim that this is evidence that state tax policy discourages rich people from living here.

This is just a measurement, but what is the context? Well, we could ask what the comparison used to be. In 2001, the comparable numbers were 3.18% and 1.67%. In other words, if this measurement means what the critics claim, Rhode Island has improved since 2001, while Massachusetts hasn't. Clearly, whatever we're doing is working, so why stop?

But to be honest about it, a movement this small over such a short time is likely just an insignificant data wobble. So, using

IRS data, I went back to 1961, and looked at the percentage of earners reporting incomes above $25,000. And it turns out that in 1961, Rhode Island and Massachusetts had roughly equivalent proportions of people that rich, 1.28% and 1.27% respectively.

So is it true? Are we chasing rich people away? Well, consider the evidence from 1972. The IRS had stopped publishing the fine grain data available a few years before, but the coarse data available implies that the modern pattern had been established, and that Massachusetts already had proportionally more wealthy people than Rhode Island. This was only a year after the establishment of Rhode Island's income tax, and though it was quite controversial at the time, it strains credulity to blame the movement on that tax change: it's a lot of people to move in a single year.

So what else had happened in the 1960's? Well, the establishment of the interstate highway system, the urban riots and school integration had all done their share to trigger the epochal flight to the suburbs that historians will note was the greatest demographic change of the 20th century. That's what. Before that point, rich people lived *in* the cities; the country was for rubes. Providence was rich, East Greenwich poor. After that point, they didn't. And like all states (except Kansas) Rhode Island contains all the cities in it. But our little state doesn't contain all its suburbs. Seekonk and Rehoboth gained from Providence's loss, along with Barrington and Warwick.

The flight from the cities was triggered by race, by crime (and fear of crime), but also by taxes. People noticed that they got more for their money beyond the borders of the cities, and as they left, the shrinking tax base made it harder for those left behind to pay for services. In other words, yes, the statistic does indicate that state tax policy drove rich people away, but it's the property tax that did it, long before the income tax was an issue.[10]

Is the income tax an issue now? Certainly some would claim it is. But by far the most affluent zip codes in the Providence metropolitan area are 02806, 02818 and 02906 (Barrington, East Greenwich, and the East Side of Providence), safely within Rhode Island's borders (IRS data). The concentration of rich people in

---

[10]In fact, the establishment of the income tax was in part a response to this very trend, as it became increasingly clear that the cities were losing their ability to finance services. Governor John Chafee campaigned for the income tax in the belief that it was a fairer tax than the property tax. Of course he lost his governorship over the issue, but since has been proven correct many times over.

Seekonk is about the same as in North Kingstown. In other words, this statistic by itself might seem to suggest that we're chasing rich people away, but the rest of the evidence tends to suggest that this statistic is essentially a side effect of the suburbanization of America and the unfortunate outcome of the borders set by our seventeenth century charter from King Charles II.

Blaming shortsighted state tax policy for the situation is, in a way, correct. But the diagnosis most often made has things exactly backwards. Rather than cut the income tax more, we should use it as it was intended, to relieve the tax pressure on our urban core cities.

Those greedy teachers

Another oft-heard statistic is that Rhode Island's teachers are more highly-paid than any others, relative to the state's median wage. One can't discount the statistic, but one can look a bit more closely at it. The median wage is the wage earned by the people in the middle of the wage scale. "Scandalous salaries" on page 105 presented data showing that professional jobs in Rhode Island pay wages a bit lower, but roughly comparable to similar jobs in Massachusetts and Connecticut, while blue-collar professions tend to pay a lot less here than in either of our neighboring states. Our architects, accountants and veterinarians are, like those in Massachusetts and Connecticut, among the highest-paid in the country. But our cashiers, locksmiths, painters and hairdressers are paid far less.

What this means is that the median wage in our state means something very different than the median wage in the neighboring states simply because the distribution of jobs and wages looks different in the three states. This is similar to the example of the school given above. The average height of the students in an all-male college means something different than the average height of the students in a co-ed school. In the all-male school, one will likely find many students who are themselves near the average height. In the other school, with the average made up of a group of taller men and another group of shorter women, it's just as likely that almost no one will be right at the average. (See Figure 8.1.)

This is important when trying to decide how easily a new student will fit in. Consider two colleges whose students have an average height of 5'6" and a new student who is 6'0". In the all-male

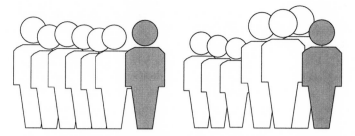

Figure 8.1: The shaded figure is slightly taller than the average in both crowds. But this means something different in the left crowd than it does in the right.

school, the new guy would seem quite tall, much taller than the average, while in the co-ed school, he would be likely to fit right in, probably around the same size as the average male. Roughly the same situation occurs when comparing teachers to the median wage in different states. In some states, teachers fit right into the overall wage distribution, while in others (like ours) they only fit comfortably into a portion of it.

We live in a small state, as is endlessly pointed out. Professionals like teachers are players in a market large enough to include substantial parts of our neighboring states. A teacher who lives in Lincoln is as likely to look for a job in Sharon or Danielson as in Cumberland or Warwick. Teaching jobs are good ones, worth commuting or moving for. Cumberland and Providence need to pay salaries comparable to nearby towns in order to attract good applicants to their jobs. This is nothing more than a fact of the job market, illustrated no better than by the legion of private employers who have made essentially the same decisions about hiring architects and accountants. The relation between teacher salaries and our state's peculiar income distribution is an indictment of the income distribution, not the teacher salaries.

Those lazy welfare recipients

So what are we to make of Rhode Island's exploding social service costs? The conventional tale is that our rules are too permissive: people stay on welfare longer here than most other places, the benefits are too rich and so on. But this diagnosis overlooks some important facts.

For one thing, a 2006 report from the Department of Human

Services[11] shows that the number of people receiving Family In-
dependence Program (FIP) cash assistance has declined dramatically since 1997, from 18,815 families to 12,074. During that time,
as families have enrolled and then left the program, over 30,000
have left welfare for work. The state's cost to support those families has declined from $51.5 million to $13.3 million. Even the
average cost of supporting an individual family has declined from
$457 per month to $418 per month. It is completely untrue to claim
that cash benefit recipients are the cause of the spending increase,
but people who discuss decreasing time limits on FIP to control
costs are implicitly claiming exactly that.

There is a claim afoot that, as other states increase the strin-
gency of their welfare requirements, poor people are streaming
into our state to take advantage of our still-permissive welfare
laws. The DHS report does point out that 9.5% of new FIP families
have, indeed, come from other states. DHS is not rigorous about
verifying this data; it's self-reported on application forms. However, the same measurement in 1996 showed 17% coming in from
other states. We don't sanction people from elsewhere, meaning
there is no incentive to lie about this, so apparently fewer people are coming into Rhode Island under the new laws than came
in before welfare reform. People who claim otherwise imagine
their hunches about the world are better sources of truth than
actual data.

So where's the spending growth? It's in services provided instead of cash benefits. If you're poor in Rhode Island, you are
eligible for assistance in health care, child care, food stamps and
more.[12] The demand for these services has skyrocketed, but a fast
growing part of the demand is for child care (doubled since 1996)
which is only subsidized for FIP recipients—and people who work.
This implies that much of the increase is just the outcome of poor
pay for blue-collar work: lots of jobs simply can't feed a family.

There is a legitimate point to be made here that aid like food
stamps or the Earned Income Tax Credit are subsidies to those
companies whose wages are too low to live on. In effect, the
state is making the already cheap cost of blue-collar labor even

---

[11] *www.dhs.ri.gov/dhs/reports/fip_2006.pdf*

[12] This is exactly the shift from cash aid to the poor that was the centerpiece
of welfare reform. Helping people become independent is a good thing, but only
people who weren't counting carefully thought child care and job training would
save money over simple cash benefits.

cheaper: welfare metamorphosed into a corporate subsidy. An economist would blame these subsidies for the low wages, while others might reverse the equation and blame the low wages for the demand for subsidies. This kind of chicken-and-egg debate is time-consuming and fairly pointless. Whichever side is correct about ultimate causation, the fact remains that hundreds of thousands of Rhode Island residents depend on these services, and sudden cutbacks will be ruinous to them, and have a tremendous ripple effect throughout our economy. And thousands of companies depend on the low wages they pay their employees. Some of these could afford to do otherwise (Wal-Mart comes to mind) but others cannot. Weaning either group from this support will be difficult and take time. But it will not happen so long as all the blame falls on the people who need food, shelter and medicine in order to live.

But won't they leave?

The public policy debate in Rhode Island seems to be organized around the principle that any increase in our income taxes will cause a hemorrhage of rich people fleeing the state. Presumably havoc will then ensue. To put it mildly, this is bizarre.

There were 12,900 people who lived in Rhode Island and reported more than $200,000 income on their 2006 taxes. Will they all leave? The president of Brown is among them. If income taxes were to increase, she wouldn't leave, and if she did, Brown would hire someone else, who would earn around the same income. Ditto the presidents of Blue Cross and Rhode Island Hospital. The Governor is probably also among the elect. Will he leave?

An interesting paper by economists Thomas Pinketty and Emmanual Saez[13] shows that the top of the income scale in English-speaking countries around the world is now occupied by wage-earners, instead of rentiers. That is, it's CEOs, not capitalists, who are now our ruling class. The important thing about that is that these are people who work *at* some company or other. In other words, the majority of the 9,000 richest Rhode Islanders are probably the owners or presidents of the Rhode Island enterprises that made them rich. What makes us think a tax hike will cause a catastrophic number of them to abandon our state and the businesses that made their fortune?

---

[13]National Bureau of Economic Research, Working Paper 11955, January 2006.

It's as certain as anything can be that an income tax hike will cause some wealthy people to leave. No doubt at least one of them will catch the ear of an enterprising *Providence Journal* reporter, and we'll get to read about their travails in gory detail. Coverage of that case and the endless pious discussion in editorials and conferences will then be allowed to obscure the actual migration rate, which will probably be as modest as the tax changes proposed.

The real question isn't whether a tax change will cause some rich people to leave. Of course it will. But continually decaying schools and expensive housing will cause some rich people to leave, too. What's more, this second effect has already happened—and is still happening, as the original suburbs are displaced by further-out suburbs. As the rich once fled Providence for Barrington and Warwick, now they don't stop before East Greenwich or Narragansett, Again, poor schools and high property taxes were among the important original reasons for rich flight to the suburbs. It's late to be addressing this, but better late than never.

Nine

Disrupting Convention

Immigrants R Us

Putting immigration and its costs into perspective.

April 2008

L ENNY BRUCE USED TO SAY he didn't believe the stories about dolphins pushing drowning sailors to shore. He said dolphins just like to push people around—and you never hear from the people who get pushed *away* from land.

As a nation of immigrants, we hear a familiar line whenever immigration comes up: "My grandparents came here and they worked hard and they did fine." And whenever I hear it, I think of a Greek uncle of mine, Niko, who I knew when I was little. He wasn't strictly related, but he was married to Georgia, my aunt's best friend, and frequently showed up at family holidays where I played with his daughter Photini. Niko never really mastered English, and I remember him sitting quietly by himself somewhere to the side of the action during those holiday gatherings. Sometime around when I was 16, Georgia died and he decided that America just wasn't for him, and moved back to Athens.

I think of Niko because my grandparents came here and they worked hard and did, well, okay. But some of their friends came here, worked hard, and didn't do well at all. Those people didn't marry, or they moved back to Greece, or they fell sick and died. We have to remember that the people who speak so proudly of their grandparents are the descendants of the winners, but that doesn't mean there weren't losers. Unfortunately, like the swimmers nudged away from shore, we never hear from them because they don't have boastful grandchildren around to even out the immigration debate with tales of their ancestors' failure.

And here's the other remarkable thing about these debates. The first half of the 20th century was a hard time in this country. Franklin Roosevelt talked about a "third of a nation, ill-housed, ill-clad, ill-nourished," and that was a time that defeated a lot of people, almost including my family, too. My grandfather, who came here when he was 10 to be a water boy on the railroads, lost his Chicago real estate business in 1929, opened a grocery store, lost that, moved to Massachusetts, where my grandmother's family was, and opened a bar with the little capital he had left. Then he died. Things were pretty rough during the 1930's, and it's amazing to me that people can look back on that time and wish that experience on others. But when you hear people say that their grandparents made it despite the hardships, so why can't modern immigrants, isn't that what they're saying?

These days, we have around 12 million people in the US illegally, and somewhere between 20,000 and 40,000 in Rhode Island. The Federation for American Immigration Reform (FAIR), which seems to be where lots of these numbers come from, estimates 35,000 and that that the cost to Rhode Island state and local government of services to them is around $99 million each year.[1]

Well here's some news: immigrants pay taxes, but that seems to be left out of the FAIR calculations. The Congressional Budget Office (CBO) put out a report in December 2007 about the cost to state and local governments, and according to numbers I found in their footnotes and articles they referenced, our 35,000 undocumented immigrants probably pay around $30 million in sales tax, around $5 million in income tax and around $40 million in property taxes (mostly via rent).

This doesn't add up to the whole $99 million, but part of the $24 million difference is offset by federal dollars that help pay for many of these services. Taking that into account, and acknowledging that all these numbers are fairly rough[2] it still seems like undocumented immigrants cost us money, but not nearly enough for the full-throated screams you hear on the radio.

But notice this: the state seems to come out ahead in these calculations, but not the cities and towns. FAIR estimates that $87 million out of the $99 million is the expense of educating im-

---

[1]FAIR is an alarmist group, and all of their numbers seem high to me, as if they've assumed the maximum wherever a range is possible, but let's go with them for the sake of argument.

[2]It's always hard to measure illegal activity, so no one has exact figures.

migrants' children. $40 million in property taxes won't cover that. The flip side of this coin is that by FAIR's numbers, the state is only incurring $12 million in expenses, and getting $35 million. The Governor's response? Cut state services.

In a way, this mirrors the situation with the federal government. According to the CBO report again, the federal government gains quite a bit more from undocumented immigrants than they cost. (An immigrant with a forged Social Security card isn't ever going to get Social Security benefits.) But the federal government hasn't shared that boon with the states, who just have to suffer for the poor immigration policy choices made at the higher level. Meanwhile, at the state level, the state government also seems to come out ahead. Down at the bottom of the pecking order, the cities and towns once again get the shaft. Both the federal and state governments benefit by having another government down the line on which they can load the burdens and refuse to share the benefits.

Policy failures at the federal level have (once again) created a fiscal problem for the states. Policy failures at the state level have created a fiscal problem for cities and towns. But people like the Governor, who are responsible for those failures, want us to get mad at immigrants instead of at them. The mystery is why we go along with it.

No accounting for reality

Sometimes the most profound impacts on our lives stem from banal and astonishingly boring rule changes unnoted at the time. The 2006 accounting rule changes were not only such a moment, but they illustrate nicely the perils of analyzing government spending with rules designed for corporations.

January 2006

L URKING IN THE OFFING of the 2007 budget are some profound changes in the rules about how governments account for some expenses. These national rule changes are going to raise all our taxes, for no good reason, and constitute a kind of cosmic joke at the expense of politicians who espouse "conservative" economic views. Before discussing the new rules, it's worth introducing the rule-makers.

The Financial Accounting Standards Board (FASB) is a group of accountants brought together in 1973 to establish the rules of corporate accounting on behalf of the federal Securities and Exchange Commission. There is a lot of discretion involved in accounting expenses at some corporation—is this expense a current expense or a capital expense? Is that payment from routine business practices, or is it a windfall? FASB was established to standardize many of these decisions. They publish a set of guidelines called the Generally Accepted Accounting Principles (GAAP), and these are what accountants use to audit corporations (and to run them).

These accounting principles are not universal. Insurance companies and banks are businesses that require rules that differ from the GAAP. When you give an insurance company some premium money, you enter into a different relationship with that company than when you give some money to a cleaning service, and deposits at a bank are a different matter still. You could run an insurance company with accounting principles meant for a cleaning service, but when you wanted to ask important questions like "Are we making money?" or "What should our premiums be?" the answers would be misleading. Therefore, there is an entirely different set of accounting principles for insurance companies, developed by the National Association of Insurance Commissioners, and yet another for banks, developed by the Federal Reserve.

Accounting rules are all about the portrayal of reality, but they are not reality. If you were a landlord making some repair to a house you rent, you might classify that repair to be a maintenance expense, or it might be big enough that you might decide it was really a capital expense. One choice will lead to a certain set of actions, while the other choice will lead to a different set. Deciding that it was a capital expense means that you might depreciate its cost over several years when you go to calculate your income tax, while a maintenance cost can be deducted right away. But neither choice makes any difference at all to the roofing company who did the work; they only want to be paid. How you choose to portray the expense may make a difference to you going forward, but it doesn't affect the underlying reality of the transaction.

You can also taste the arbitrary flavor of the rules in the way that even under the GAAP principles, there are two systems. A company can account for its expenses when the payment is actually made (the "cash" system) or when it is promised to a supplier ("accrual"). Some accountants prefer one system over another, but the two are both valid portrayals of a business.

With all this background, let's introduce the Government Accounting Standards Board, founded in 1984. GASB is another private group of accountants associated with FASB, whose job it is to establish accounting rules for governments. The GASB rules are widely adhered to,[3] and auditors refer to them while conducting their audits. GASB has recently made two important changes in accounting procedures that will have essentially similar effects: Statements 43 and 45. These will require that as of 2008, governments account for the costs of health and other benefits they pay to their retirees in the same way that they account for pension costs.[4]

These rulings say that the expense of providing some post-employment benefit was incurred when the employee earned it. This sounds reasonable, but the practical effect is that unless a government plans to fund these future expenses out of investment income, *and* already has the funds put aside for that purpose, it must show an "unfunded liability" for the future amount on their books today. Towns, cities and states who will be perfectly capable of paying these expenses in the future will appear to have budgets in deep deficit. The accounting change will make Rhode Island's 2008 budget appear to be in a $629 million hole that isn't there in 2007.

Funding this kind of expense out of investment income is obviously desirable. But like many obviously good ideas, there are hidden factors that complicate the picture.

By the calculation of our actuaries, as of 2006, Rhode Island has a $629 million unfunded liability due to its promises to fund the health insurance of state retirees. This is the present value of our promises, estimated out a few decades or so. This is a lot of money, but in a just world, there would be several different ways we could choose to address this problem. We could figure out some way to put aside $629 million and invest it, and fund the costs from the investment income. This will inevitably mean big tax hikes, big service cuts, or big luck. Or we could fund the ever-

---

[3]But not universally. The U.S. government has its own rules, and does not follow GASB rules for capital expenses.

[4]See "The truth about unfunded liabilities" on page 32 for more about public pension costs

increasing amount out of tax revenue, which is what we do now. Or we could invest $629 million in the education of our children, or in our universities, and allow the resulting growth in our economy to cover the added costs. Or we could take the hint, realizing that it's more than just state retirees who are having health insurance problems, and spend $629 million to create an equitable and just universal health care system that saves money for all of us. Or we could leave the money in our citizens' pockets for now, and and figure that the growth in personal income over time will be more than enough to pay the cost when the bill comes due. But according to GASB, only the first of these will do, and the Governor plans to meekly knuckle under. After all, according to the accountants, money spent on education is only an expense, not an investment.

By demanding strict adherence to their definition of fiscal prudence, GASB—an unelected, private group of accountants in Connecticut—insists that our government *not* act to solve our problems in any way that they didn't think of already. To their credit, GASB does say that Statements 43 and 45 don't demand that the unfunded liability must be paid off, only that it be shown clearly on financial statements. But they don't have to demand it. When the "liability" appears on the state's balance sheet, people like the Governor demand it be paid off.

The secret joke in all this is that self-proclaimed economic conservatives, like the Governor, don't object to these GASB rules, even though their implication is that funding government expenses in a "fiscally prudent" manner is a higher good than the economic growth possible by leaving this money in private hands. Governments do more than collect and spend money. Some of what they do is actually helpful to people, and some is also helpful to economic growth. Unlike any corporation, a government has a claim on the income of its citizens, and this means that a far wider variety of useful investment is possible. The future of any government depends on the future income of its citizens and—as is endlessly pointed out in other situations—it is in the best interests of a government to act to increase that future income.

But the GASB rules effectively demand that governments raise taxes in the near term, rather than leave the money in the hands of individuals and businesses who might invest it in other ways. Defending this kind of accounting is a curious position for a protector of the free market to take.

The costs of guessing about crime

It is unremarkable by now to hear about policing methods that use profiles or other actuarial methods to predict likely criminals. What most don't realize is that there is a social cost to actuarial methods like these, especially now that they've become so common. This is a book review of Against Prediction, *by Bernard Harcourt (2007).*

October 2007

S UPPOSE YOU WALK through the fish markets in southern Spain, and observe lots of sea bass and very little cod. What do you infer from that? Probably that sea bass outnumber the cod in local waters. As it turns out, though, the sea bass are in the Mediterranean, and the cod in the Atlantic and the imbalance is the result of a preference for fishing in calmer waters. The fish in the market are there in those proportions because of fishing strategy, not because of their populations. Bernard E. Harcourt, a professor at the University of Chicago law school, uses this and similar stories about arrest rates and racial profiling, to illustrate his assault on common strategies among 21st century police and prisons. His chief target: the practice of predicting who will be a criminal.

Prediction techniques are by now quite common in law enforcement, and are used to allocate police resources, to dictate sentences and to make parole and probation decisions. They involve gathering statistics from past offenders and neighborhood trouble spots, and using them to develop profiles of likely criminals. Harcourt's argument, roughly rendered, is this: There is at least a little crime everywhere, so in a very real way, you'll find crime wherever you look. So if you mostly look in minority neighborhoods, that's mostly where you'll find it. Imagine a world with 20% orange drivers, and the rest green, and imagine that 10% of the orange drivers are carrying illegal drugs, and 8% of everyone else. There is a disparity, but it's not a big one.[5] Now imagine that the police begin an aggressive program to search orange drivers, devoting half their resources to them. Eventually word gets out that orange drivers are at risk and green drivers are safe. If drivers are rational[6] then the crime rate among orange drivers will go down

---

[5]Especially in a world with such high crime rates. Remember this is just a fantasy world used for an illustration.

[6]See "The spectre of rationality" on page 146.

as the risk of arrest goes up. Say it goes down to 9%. Unfortunately, it's also likely that the rest of the world will notice, and the offending rate among the green drivers might go up, say to 9%. There are lots more of them, so now you've actually got *more* crime than you had before the policing began.

What you also have is statistics to "prove" that orange drivers are responsible for half the crimes. After all, they make up half the arrests, don't they? In this regime, an orange offender is more than three times as likely to be arrested than a green one.

Now, using these arrest statistics, we develop a profile of who is most likely to be arrested again after being released from jail. Since oranges are far more likely to be arrested, the statistics are likely to show them far more likely to be re-arrested. So obviously we should be less eager to offer them parole, right?

But look what's happened: A series of seemingly sensible policing and incarceration policies have led to an increase in crime and a tremendous disparity in arrests and sentencing policy. Sometimes "seemingly sensible" just isn't good enough.

To wind up with a world like this, we only assumed that the offense rate among the minority was slightly higher than that for everyone else, but Harcourt also shows that the system drives to the same outcomes, no matter what the actual starting point. The only requirements are the *perception* that crime is more prevalent among some minority group than it is in the majority, and that groups change their behavior according to the degree of police attention. Essentially, you can't police a community without having the biases of the police force affect it.

Strategies like these are quite common, and have become an everyday part of our justice system. Three-strikes laws, parole policies and police resource choices all depend on these kinds of predictions. To Harcourt, what's at least as troubling as this is that the effects of these strategies have shifted our attitudes about what exactly justice *is*. It was once thought that equal punishment for equal crimes constituted a just system, but now we have people who will claim that justice demands that certain classes of people deserve harsher punishment for the same crimes. Laws that automatically put repeat offenders away for life for minor crimes, are a perfect example. This is not how we used to define justice.

Statistics run amok

Unfortunately, after a powerful indictment of prediction practices, Harcourt's analysis misses some facts about how we use statistics and then goes astray on his recommendations for the future. He accurately points out that assessing the amount of crime by analyzing arrest records inevitably lets the biases of the police leak into the analysis. To analyze crime, it is true that what you really want—and can't get—is statistics about how much crime happens, not statistics about how much is detected. What's at least as important, though, is what you do with the data you get. There is a fundamental difference between the use of statistics in science and the use of statistics by insurance actuaries. It's central to the problems Harcourt identifies, but he misses it.

When actuaries compile their data to prove that young men are poor risks for auto insurers, they do not claim that there is anything about being a boy that makes you a bad driver. Instead, the claim is that being a boy in 21st-century America entails a bunch of other facts—some known, some unknown—some of which cause unsafe driving. Being a boy is a good *marker* for unsafe driving, but it isn't a *cause*, strictly speaking. A marker has two important properties: it must have a good correlation to risk, and it must be easy to see. Insurance companies find it convenient to use the sex marker in setting their auto premiums, simply because determining sex is easier than determining a driver's general level of responsibility or likelihood of being out late with friends.[7]

Contrast this with researchers in science. Psychologists looking into questions about learning to read may look at correlations between a mother's education and a child's achievement, not because they think that the one is a good marker for the other, but because they hypothesize that the one is a possible cause of the other.[8] The statistics these researchers develop are a way to test this hypothesis. A decent correlation is an invitation for further research to look at exactly what's going on, but the researchers don't conclude that the correlation means anything by itself.

---

[7]There are cases where a marker can be a cause, such as a waterfront home having a higher risk of flooding, but these are only coincidences whose contrast with the other cases proves the point.

[8]See, for example, *Unfulfilled Expectations: Home and School Influences on Literacy*, by Catherine Snow, et al., Harvard University Press, 1991.

There are some superficial similarities between these two activities. Both use sophisticated statistics and sampling strategies and both report their findings in terms of carefully couched probabilities, but at root, these are fundamentally different enterprises. The actuaries are looking for correlations good enough to predict the future, and the scientists are using the good correlations they find to uncover new facts.

The difference is in the application. Where a correlation is used to penalize members of some group, we want to know that there is a cause to link the group and the property. For example, being black and smoking are both associated with shortened life expectancies. Basing life insurance premiums on smoking has been done for years, while basing premiums on race can only be done covertly, when it is done at all. Intuitively, we see one as just and the other unjust.

Using markers instead of causes reliably produces unjust results, because it classifies people by what they are instead of what they do. In some cases, the potential injustices (overcharging safe-driving boys, undercharging reckless girls) are small, so we tolerate them. In the cases Harcourt writes about, the statistics are used to determine punishments, and the stakes are far higher. When you're talking about sending someone to prison—or worse—there are no small injustices.

Where from here?

If statistical reasoning can't help us in matters of crime prevention, what do we do? Harcourt suggests that the only fair policing strategies involve random sampling. In a purely technical sense, this is absolutely correct. The only reliable way to get the prison population to reflect the population at large is probably to police randomly.

Unfortunately, this cure seems worse than the disease. In the post-9/11 world, our nation already seems to be creeping slowly towards a world where everyone is under surveillance all the time. It is difficult to understand how anyone but an academic worrying about statistics could imagine that adding a regime of random scrutiny to our society might be a good idea. In the past week, I've had to empty my pockets for a visit to the State House library and as a chaperone on a grade school field trip to Ellis Island. We don't really know the extent to which the government has been spying on all of us, but what little evidence is available tells us it's not been modest. The "war on terror" has already left Fourth Amendment strictures against searches without cause lying in tatters. Do we have to burn the remnants to fight crime?

Probably not. Harcourt imagines that there are only two alternatives: profiling and random sampling. But it won't be possible for police to patrol without using their experience and hunches to predict what might happen and who might do it. Police officers are human, and demanding that they ignore their experience seems akin to Canute ordering back the tide. Harcourt's research shows us that a system that isn't aware of the limitations of these tools can expect bad racial outcomes. Instead of ditching the system, we can work to make it aware of the limitations. Instead of designing a police regime to deliver a randomly sampled prison population, how about working toward a regime where racial imbalances are widely seen—within and without the police establishment—as evidence of discrimination, and where police seek to fix that discrimination rather than defend it?

We need to talk about restoring justice to our system of justice. The sad truth is that there are a tremendous number of people in America who perceive the justice system as oppressive and unjust. Much research shows that beliefs in the legitimacy and effectiveness of law enforcement are the two most important determinants of whether someone obeys the law,[9] *and* that legitimacy stems from a basic sense of whether the system is fair and respectful. It's not all about outcomes, but whether people think the system gives them a fair shake. In this respect it's hard to argue that the system hasn't failed large numbers of people in Rhode Island.

Ten-year prison sentences for possessing an ounce of drugs, the abandonment of the assumption of innocence in parole violation hearings and the use of excessive force all contribute to a weakening of the legitimacy of law enforcement. We can use Harcourt's findings to work toward restoring the legitimacy of law enforcement without trying to get police officers to roll dice before making a search.

---

[9]See Tom Tyler, for example, *Why People Obey the Law*, Yale University Press, 1990. (Reissued in 2006 by Princeton University Press.) See chapter 5 especially, and Tyler and Huo, *Trust in the law: Encouraging public cooperation with the police and courts*, Russell Sage Fdn, 2002.

The spectre of rationality

Almost all theoretical analyses of crime and punishment (including Harcourt's) are committed to the idea that we exist in a universe of rational people. Despite everyday evidence of irrational people, academics refuse to give up the concept because to do so would imply that society is forever beyond the reach of the analytical tools of science.

Few want to give up so easily, so there have been some promising advances. For example, economist Daniel Kahneman won a Nobel prize for his work with Amos Tversky describing a kind of "bounded rationality" where people are mostly rational, but seldom have all the information they need, and use shortcuts and beliefs in their reasoning that create not-entirely-rational outcomes. Their work is fundamental to the field of behavioral economics, which tries to incorporate psychological insights into economic models.

As a way to salvage rationality from the evidence against it, this isn't bad, but it still misses the real problem: The tools are good but inadequate. A social scientists who uses rational choice models to study human society resembles a meteorologist equipped with a box of plastic bags with which to study clouds. This is true even when the models attempt to incorporate modifications to rationality.

In other words, running drugs is irrational, unless it's important as a favor to keep peace with the gang you've decided is crucial to your life because they run your neighborhood, and you don't want to be beaten up or worse on your way to school. Going to a better school is rational, unless it's hard to get to because your mother's job is in the opposite direction, and her sister just died so she had to miss the application deadline in order to attend the funeral and hunt through her sister's things for the jewelry she knows their mother left her. Getting a better job is rational, unless your current job allows you the flexibility to pursue your career as a sculptor, which your husband pushes you to pursue due to the guilt he feels over his sister, who choked to death on a defective saxophone reed at a party to celebrate her first recording contract. Even if people are mostly rational, or boundedly rational, typical academic analyses of our lives are so superficial that they can't possibly get at the dark and tangled Amazonian jungle of social rewards and penalties that we all hack our way through each day.

Social scientists who have looked into this question have made some interesting findings. A lovely paper by Courtney Bell[10] argues that part of the reason school choice programs seem not to work is that the people who design them don't anticipate the breadth of concerns that typical parents and students have. Academic excellence is important, but rating it as #2 on the priority list is not evidence of irrationality.

Do tax cuts shrink government?

Some surprising results about cutting taxes from the director of the libertarian Cato Institute.

June 2006

A 2006 ARTICLE by William Niskanen, the director of the libertarian Cato Institute, reviewed the idea that cutting taxes is a sensible step in reducing the size of government. [11] The theory, sometimes referred to as the "Starve the Beast" strategy, is the intellectual foundation of today's Republican party, and it's so much a part of mainstream political discourse that no one remembers a time when this kind of talk would have been thought rather odd. Back then, in the misty dawn of time, in order to cut a budget, you had to suggest something to cut. The idea that you could be *for* something as amorphous and content-free as simply paying less for government simply wasn't the done thing. You can see this in the data. In Figure 9.1, government revenues and expenses move more or less together until the 1970's. After that, they don't.

Niskanen's article attacks the theory first: according to orthodox price economics, price controls are a bad thing because when you artifically lower the price of something, people demand more than they would otherwise. Running deficits is something akin to artifically lowering the price of government, so according to this theory, people will ask for more government, not less. Niskanen expresses some surprise that such advocates of price theory as economist Milton Friedman would endorse "Starve the Beast" as late as 2003.

---

[10]See "Market failure by 'irrational' behavior" on page 53.

[11]Mr. Niskanen was kind enough to share a pre-publication draft of his work, and the analysis here is drawn from that.

Why is that late? Because it was almost 30 years ago that some people began to promote the idea that one could be thought intellectually respectable while proposing to cut taxes spending without suggesting what spending to cut. Instead of shrinking government by cutting programs, the idea was simply to shrink it by cutting taxes, and letting the pressure of tight budgets do the job for you. The tax revolts in California and Massachusetts were just such campaigns. Neither campaign was really based on a critique of what government did, just how much it cost, and leaders in both campaigns spoke in generalities about "doing with less" and "creating efficiency" that allowed any listener to imagine that the services they valued would continue to be provided (often falsely). Neither campaign dealt with the inconvenient details, but both were highly successful in rallying voters, and Ronald Reagan took note, and so did the people who crafted his budgets.

For better or worse, the date of this revolution means that we now have a quarter century of actual budget data. We can answer the questions in terms of practice, not just theory. So does it work? In a nutshell: no. Niskanen did some statistical analyses of these numbers which allowed him to correct for the outside effects of the interest rates and the unemployment rate, which both have an effect on the federal budget independent of government policy.

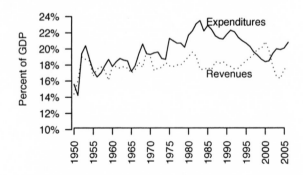

Figure 9.1: *The dotted line is federal government outlays as a percent of GDP, and the solid line is revenues. Postwar, the two tracked fairly closely until 1970 (and a bit further, if you discount the effects of the unemployment rate and interest rate on federal spending). Since then—strange as it sounds—spending declines when taxes are rising and vice versa. (Source: Economic Report of the President)*

Even after these corrections, the answer is still no.

A surprise was hiding in the details. Not only doesn't it work to starve the beast, but after controlling for changes in unemployment and interest rates, it seems that the relation between federal revenues and expenditure growth since Reagan is actually *negative*. Since 1980, as taxes have fallen, spending has risen, and when taxes have risen, spending has fallen. This sounds very odd, but it's true. Reagan and the Bushes have given us bigger government with higher deficits, and Clinton gave us smaller government with a surplus. To be fair, this is an over-simple analysis, concentrating on gross measures, like total federal spending, which don't reflect some important detail. But when the theoretical analysis is backed up with the practical record, it becomes a compelling counter-argument, even from this kind of bird's-eye view.

Niskanen's argument is about the relation between government expenditure *growth* and taxes, but you can see a similar story in the simple relation between expenditure and revenue, which is also negative since 1980, after discounting unemployment and interest rates. With this measure, I found several long periods with significant positive correlations before 1980,[12] but remarkably, I found no other period after 1901 with a significant negative relationship—not during the Great Depression, nor during the World Wars, nor during the Cold War—none.

In other words, before Reagan, there was wide agreement about how to handle government finances. Certainly the government ran deficits, but in general, revenues and expenses traveled in the same direction. When spending went up, taxes went up to pay for it, though perhaps not as fast. When revenue went down, spending was cut, though perhaps not as fast.

Figure 9.2 illustrates the sea change. The solid line shows federal spending as a percentage of GDP from 1980 to 2005, and the dotted line shows revenue, just as in Figure 9.1. The new dashed

---

[12] Budget data for this analysis came from the Economic Report of the President. GDP and interest rates are from the Economic History web site (*eh.net*), and articles there by Lawrence Officer, "What Was the Interest Rate Then" (2003) and Louis D. Johnston and Samuel H. Williamson, "The Annual Real and Nominal GDP for the United States, 1790–Present" (2005). The historic unemployment rates are from the Bureau of Labor Statistics, back to 1929. Before that, unemployment did not have much effect on the federal budget, since there were so few federal social insurance programs.

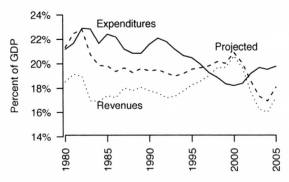

Figure 9.2: A close-up of the last 25 years shown in Figure 9.1. The dashed line labeled "Projected" shows what Presidents before Reagan might have done with the revenue we received. Of course they'd have done everything else differently, too, so this is just for the sake of argument. (Niskanen's projections.)

line shows Niskanen's analysis of what federal spending would have been if the presidents since 1980 had conformed to the post-war norms until then, depending on revenue, the unemployment rate and interest rates. According to his analysis, where a president like Eisenhower would have lowered federal spending by a lot in the 1980's, it didn't decline nearly as fast under Reagan or Bush Senior. Where a Kennedy might have increased spending in the 1990's to take advantage of rising revenues, Clinton cut spending dramatically to lower the deficit.

According to this analysis, seems that what is now thought to be good electoral strategy really was once upon a time widely thought to be too cynical for polite company. Niskanen shows us that Eisenhower didn't govern this way, Truman didn't, and neither, apparently, did Kennedy, or Johnson or any other 20th century president. "Cynical" is a character trait once thought to define Richard Nixon, but his "secret plan" was about the war, not taxes.

Starve the Beast isn't just questionable theory and a disingenuous lack of specifics. The data tell the story: with a quarter-century's experience, we can say that there is a fundamental dishonesty associated with campaigns that promise to "cut taxes" but won't tell us what programs are to go in order to pay for the cuts. Campaigns this simple promise what they can't deliver, and the candidates who get elected this way deliver the opposite of what they promise. The result is government bankrupted and unable to perform even the uncontroversial functions well.

This isn't only a national phenomenon. Rhode Island can't run a deficit in the current fiscal year, but we can run a deficit *next* year, which isn't a problem until then, and state government does that all the time. The recently passed 2007 state budget does exactly this, via a huge tax cut for the wealthiest Rhode Islanders that won't have its full impact until 2011. Inappropriate borrowing, like at the Department of Transportation, contributes, too.

Using tricks like these, Rhode Island governors are free to be as fiscally irresponsible as any president, and they and the Assembly have made the most of it, constantly promising lower taxes. And when they propose a program cut, and it fails or is modified in the legislature, somehow the taxes get cut anyway. The 2006 budget year is a perfect example. The flat tax cut for the rich will cost $7.5 million in fiscal 2007, but more than ten times that five years later. Needless to say, no corresponding program cuts were made; that's a problem for legislators in 2010.

Our experience, nationally and locally, shows us that promising lower taxes without being specific is both ineffective at achieving the stated goals and very effective at getting candidates elected. But airy promises to lower taxes can only be an effective campaign strategy when people think the candidate making the promises is serious. When Ronald Reagan ran for president, people took him seriously. The press wrote respectfully about him, and Republican party activists and writers supported him and lacerated those who tried to call attention to the non-serious aspects of his platform (like George Bush, Senior, who memorably called Reagan's economic analysis "voodoo economics"). But the truth is that in fiscal matters Reagan was spouting nonsense, and Niskanen's analysis is just one more piece of evidence. That he—along with subsequent candidates for national and state offices around the country—was allowed by the press and the public to masquerade as a serious candidate is to our lasting detriment.

It's a complex world, and it's no surprise that people rely on the opinions of others to form their own. But this reliance becomes our undoing when we allow serious-but-unconventional ideas to be mocked and the non-serious to be treated as wisdom. We rely on the press to tell us who's serious, but maybe that's not such a good idea. Be that as it may, we're now in a strange spot, where the irresponsible campaigners are rewarded with the reins of government. Whatever the responsibility for getting us here, at least remember the judgment of the director of one of the Republican party's favorite think tanks: according to theory and experience both, if what you want is smaller government, simply cutting taxes is a lousy way to get there. There's a message for tax-cutting candidates here: If you aren't brave enough to be specific about cuts, then go home and don't make things worse.

Ten

What To Do?

A S ANY PHYSICIAN KNOWS, proper diagnosis of a condition is only the first step.[1] A diagnosis is useless—sometimes worse than useless—without a therapy. In this case, a description of a possible therapy can also serve to illuminate more of the differences between the conventional tale and the view of Rhode Island's condition presented in this volume.

Here, then, is a brief and necessarily incomplete list of the kinds of policies that might address our situation. If you still believe in the conventional tale, the suggestions here may seem to fly in the face of common sense. However, if I've persuaded you that this tale is flawed in many and important ways, you may agree with me that the policies of our state seem destined to make our situation worse, and that the following ideas are worth consideration.

Mend relations between state and towns

The adversarial relationship between Rhode Island's state government and its cities and towns continues to be at the heart of our state's woes, and it continues to be widely ignored. The state complains that the towns waste money, and the towns complain that the state routinely reneges on its promises. True, there are frequent calls for a predictable education funding formula, but little progress has been made. The result has been uncontrolled suburban sprawl as towns try in vain to grow themselves out of fiscal difficulty. This serves our towns poorly and serves the cities even worse. Solving this problem will be hard, and both the state and the municipalities will have to compromise on issues of autonomy and money, but it's essential to a sane future.

---

[1]Remember that headache from Chapter One? See page 2.

Regionalize land-use planning and taxation

It is possible that regionalizing and consolidating some municipal services could be a good thing, and could even save towns some money, but the cost savings are routinely overestimated. Regionalization of taxation and land-use planning, however, has the potential to be able to clamp down on escalating costs by adjusting services to the movement of people. Paradoxically, such a system could be the best way to *preserve* local control of communities by their residents.

Under the status quo, towns feel in control of their fates, but they are not. People move to Exeter for its rural character but destroy that rural character in the act of doing so. Under the current system, the people of Exeter have no way to resist this change. Similarly, there are hundreds of jobs at risk in the redevelopment of Providence's waterfront, but the city is forced to consider the possibility simply because waterfront condos would bring in more tax revenue. This is not local control, but only the illusion of control. We need regional planning and a funding mechanism that won't doom a town to bankruptcy if it doesn't choose unbridled growth.

Reduce reliance on the property tax

Planning authority is useless when town finances depend as heavily on land development as they do here. Rhode Island's municipalities depend on ever-increasing levels of property tax in order to pay their bills. This produces pressure both on tax rates, but also on land-use decisions. Poor land-use decisions increase a town's infrastructure needs, bringing short-term cash but costing much more in the long term. We cannot continue to rely so heavily on the property tax without making our fiscal disaster worse.

We have seen that uncontrolled growth is not serving our state well—fiscally or in any other way. Reducing our reliance on the property tax is an essential step to getting our growth under control, and it is also an important step toward ending our depressive tax policy.

Restore progressivity to our tax code

Progressive taxes are not just a matter of fairness, it is also a way to keep money in the hands of people who will spend it, the most effective and efficient way to keep our economy moving. When you include the property tax in the analysis, our tax code is not—and never has been—progressive. But the changes of the past decade have made the code even less progressive, and serve to stifle our local economy just when we most need it to expand. One way to approach this is simply by ending some of the more egregious incentives and credits that litter our state tax code. But increasing progressivity will mean trading income for property taxes.

Rhode Island is a small state, and our position between two richer states obviously limits our capacity to act in many ways, not least in tax policy. Some tax changes might encourage the migration of taxpayers (or of transactions for potential changes in the sales tax). But statistics tell us the risk is lower than it is frequently claimed to be, and circumstances tell us that the risk of inaction far higher. Both are important, and widely overlooked factors in the equation.

Shrink regulatory costs and overhead

Too often, calls to alleviate permitting and paperwork burdens are made by people who simply object to the rules. After all, you can make more money as a land developer if you can get permits to build on swamps. But the transparency of such complaints can't blind us to the need to make compliance with state laws as easy and efficient as possible. Application delays need to be shortened or eliminated, and paperwork requirements must be audited to determine whether they're useful. Starting a business is already difficult enough; we must not require a business to make multiple contacts with multiple state departments just to conduct routine business.

Reform state budgeting practices

Our state is constitutionally required to balance its budget before the beginning of each fiscal year. But there is no requirement to balance the budget of the following year, and our budget-writers have abused this loophole, cutting taxes in future years, borrowing funds to be repaid in the future, and even gross shifting of expenses from one year to the next. What's more, budget writers have conspired to keep a tremendous amount of borrowing off-books, using bonds issued by quasi-public agencies, or resorting to technicalities to keep it uncounted and unbudgeted, as with the transportation GARVEE bonds (see "State debt" on page 15).

These practices must be stopped. Some form of multi-year budgeting would help immeasurably, as would refusing to respect such technicalities as counting only "tax supported" debt, since all of the state's debt is ultimately backed by our taxes.

Raise wages at the low levels

Wages in Rhode Island are comparable to neighboring states for professional jobs, but the available data suggest they are much lower than our neighbors for blue-collar work. This is a problem for our economy since financial pressures on blue-collar workers will keep the demand for goods and services lower here than in other states. Government has only limited leverage over private employers in issues like this, but is not powerless. Raising the minimum wage[2] and adopting "living wage" contract regulations are within our power.

Invest in education

The cost of education must be reframed from budget "expense" to "investment." The strength and resilience of the Massachusetts economy is ultimately attributable to little besides education, and that's a lesson we should learn. This is not a call to indulge teacher unions—the biggest cost drivers in school budgets are not of the unions' making. Unions are not to blame for health care cost inflation, our state's reckless pension funding policy or transportation and special education mandates from the state and federal governments.

Part of improving education is doing the hard work of making schools better for *all* our children, not the comparatively easy work of inventing a better school. Charter schools are fine things, and we should continue to experiment with how best to provide public education, but we also must find a way to use these experiments to benefit the majority of students who don't get to attend them, instead of penalizing them, as we do now.

Develop an effective industrial policy

It is an uncomfortable truth, but as planned-economy-ish as it sounds, our state *has* an industrial policy. For exam-

---

[2]Or indexing it to automatically rise with inflation, a step the Rhode Island Senate has already passed once.

ple, we have favored financial industries with substantial tax breaks and credits and the red carpet has been out at EDC for biotech companies. But our current industrial policy is the result of the haphazard pursuit of whatever seems to come wandering down the pike in our general direction. Worse, the levers of policy seem never to be pulled in favor of the many businesses that are already here. For example, as of the 2007 Census of Agriculture, Rhode Island's farms are a $65 million industry. We have around 1,200 farms, up 42% since 2002, and sales are up 19%. But the state does not have a coherent agricultural policy that might address such issues as having the most expensive farmland in the nation, or the conflicts that inevitably arise when suburban developments come to abut farm fields periodically treated with smelly fertilizer.

It's not good strategy to favor specific firms, but it is a good idea to favor specific industries we want, and there are a variety of ways we can do that, none of which have to do with tax breaks. For example, establishing education programs to develop the work force for an industry will both help companies *and* leave our own citizens better off.

Rhode Island needs a consensus to develop a coherent industrial policy aimed at fostering the firms we already have, incubating the firms our citizens might hope to start, encouraging them to start more, and helping them all compete in the global market.

Tame the real estate market

Part of Rhode Island's implicit industrial policy is to favor the land development and real estate speculation industries. We offer state tax breaks to developers in the form of lower tax rates on capital gains income, and it's completely routine for large developers to demand favorable tax treatment from cities and towns in the form of "tax stabilization" treaties. Even apart from the foregone revenue, this business has significant costs to the rest of us. The developer fees levied by a few towns seldom cover the costs of a new development, especially if it eventually houses families with children in the schools. The cost of extending utility services to that development is eventually borne by all the other customers of that utility. Furthermore, real estate speculation drives up

the cost of housing for all of us, and leaves the state prone
to real estate crashes, which have now come twice in twenty
years. Booms and busts are exhausting for everyone.

Investment in real estate is *not* a productive investment
in the same way that investment in a factory is. Even if
you accept the analogy between a construction site and a
factory, suburban development relies on a fast-disappearing
resource: vacant land. Our state would be well served by
some drag on the real estate market. A land gains tax, like
they have in Vermont, could make speculation less attractive
to investors, and discourage the tendency to bubble.

If we're going to favor income from real estate, it should
be income from rentals instead of sales. This would increase
the supply in the rental market by encouraging landlords to
earn their own income by maintaining and renting buildings
instead of by buying and selling them.

Sensibly excise government waste

Government owes its citizens responsible use of the dollars
it collects. But we must be honest about exactly where and
what the waste is. For example, our insane welfare regulations force us to employ 160 people just to help people fill
out the application forms. That's waste. Our aversion to hiring permanent employees has produced absurd contracting
policies that in several departments have cost us far more
than actual employees could have. That's waste, too. Needless borrowing has cost us millions in unnecessary debt service payments. Reliance on tax credits as a vehicle of public
policy have left us paying wealthy corporations and people
millions of dollars for very little in the way of public good.
Those are waste, too, and there's more.

Too often, calls to cut waste in government have led to
ineffective programs. Here's why that's important. Having only six people in an office that had 20 a year before
and who are completely swamped and unable to be effective at their jobs *is a waste of money*. Much waste in government doesn't need uncovering. It's right there in front of
your eyes: in transportation departments that can't afford
to maintain our roads, in environmental protection departments that can't do timely reviews of the permits in front of
them, in child protection services that put the state at serious

risk of having a child die in its "care" and all the rest. Trying to run programs on a shoestring isn't a terrible idea—being economical is a *good* thing—but only if we're honest when the shoestring breaks. Otherwise, government becomes more expensive and less effective, pretty much what we've achieved.

This is hardly the end of the to-do list. Environmental regulation to preserve our important economic assets as well as our health, public transit enhancements to make life less expensive for many and cleaner for all, reconstruction of the research capacity at the University of Rhode Island, reassessment of our expensive and often counter-productive anti-crime policy choices, and much more, all deserve a place on it. But life is short and the list is long. My intent is to suggest a new direction worth taking.

And suggest is what I intend here. I make no claims to received truth. This book is what a single citizen, working in his spare time, has found in his perusals of statistics and documents relevant to our state and its government. It would be shocking if there weren't ways to improve both the analysis and the recommendations. But I also know that improvements will only come from people who consider both the critique and the proposals with an open mind.

Our government is in constant evolution. We live in a hybrid economic system—not a planned economy, but not fully a free market, either. Why? Because history has brought us here. Our state regulates the markets for haircuts, architects, insurance, and more because unregulated markets simply didn't work, and brought us head lice, collapsed buildings, and insurance swindles.[3] We forget things like this at our peril.

These and other evolutionary steps were taken by identifying a problem, and then dealing with it. Progress was not made by people who refused to acknowledge a problem, or who derided the possible solutions and insulted those who offered them. Progress was made in spite of them.

---

[3] After the 1871 Chicago fire, 58 insurance companies went bust and fewer than a third of the fire insurance policies paid off. To deny the utility of insurance regulation, for example, is to deny this and the many other debacles in the insurance industry—and the legions of unpaid policyholders—in the decades following that fire. States learned from those disasters, and in the early twentieth century, instituted laws to prevent their recurrence. State regulation is the reason why property, casualty and life insurance is such a boring but profitable business these days.

The therapy for Rhode Island's current condition is not simple, and will take commitment and work, but we are far from a basket case. Ours is a state filled with resourceful, generous, committed, and hard-working people. We have natural gifts of geography, institutions and history that could serve us well, if we choose to use them wisely. The real question is, can we figure out what that means?

Ten Things You Can Do

1. Remain skeptical the next time you hear Rhode Island is the "worst" in something. Are the comparisons fair? Are the differences significant?

2. Object the next time a friend makes an snide comment about "taxes." They're not all the same.

3. Explain this alternate story to your friends. They probably haven't heard it before.

4. Learn who your elected officials are, from school board on up. And learn their email addresses, too.

5. Write—and send—letters to the editor, to your Senator, Representative, Governor, whoever. Minds don't change without hearing another story.

6. Explain these issues to your elected officials. Most of them are true believers in the conventional tale.

7. Gently correct these officials when they try to slide past your questions with conventional, but wrong, explanations.

8. When you hear someone call for lower taxes, ask how to pay for them. Ask in the same insistent way they'd ask how to pay for a new spending program.

9. Join or start a group to make your views known to those officials. Numbers speak for themselves, and the conventional tale already has strong advocates in our government.

10. Run for office. Some minds can't be changed and have to be replaced to make progress.

Index

Tom Sgouros is a freelance researcher and writer about public policy, statistics, software and assorted other technical topics. His clients range from candidates for office, to advocacy groups and Fortune 500 companies. In Rhode Island, he has done policy work with Ocean State Action, Working Rhode Island, and the Sierra Club, among several others. He edits the *Rhode Island Policy Reporter*, and writes a newspaper column that appears regularly in  ten newspapers around the state, and irregularly in several others. He has also worked as an an engineer, videographer, fire-eater, circus producer, and robot impresario. He lives with his wife and two daughters, by the seashore, on RIPTA's number 14 bus line.

photo credit: Efrem Bromberg

To order more copies of this book, or to subscribe to the Rhode Island Policy Reporter, *see **whatcheer.net**. Bulk discounts for schools or organizations are available.*

Printed in the United States
220470BV00001B/1/P

9 780982 470701